C000244807

Battleground Eu

Airfields and Airmen
Somme

Hail to the youth of England, they who dare
To face the endless perils of the air!
They fight that soon the shouts of War may cease
And o'er the world will brood the wings of Peace;
Then through the clouds will England's glory rise
Uplifted by the heroes of the skies!

Paul Bewsher 1918
The Victors of the Air

Battleground series:

Stamford Bridge & Hastings *by* Peter Marren
Wars of the Roses - **Wakefield / Towton** *by* Philip A. Haigh
Wars of the Roses - **Barnet** *by* David Clark
Wars of the Roses - **Tewkesbury** *by* Steven Goodchild
Wars of the Roses - **The Battles of St Albans** *by*
Peter Burley, Michael Elliott & Harvey Wilson
English Civil War - **Naseby** *by* Martin Marix Evans, Peter Burton
and Michael Westaway
English Civil War - **Marston Moor** *by* David Clark
War of the Spanish Succession - **Blenheim 1704** *by* James Falkner
War of the Spanish Succession - **Ramillies 1706** *by* James Falkner
Napoleonic - **Hougoumont** *by* Julian Paget and Derek Saunders
Napoleonic - **Waterloo** *by* Andrew Uffindell and Michael Corum
Zulu War - **Isandlwana** *by* Ian Knight and Ian Castle
Zulu War - **Rorkes Drift** *by* Ian Knight and Ian Castle
Boer War - **The Relief of Ladysmith** *by* Lewis Childs
Boer War - **The Siege of Ladysmith** *by* Lewis Childs
Boer War - **Kimberley** *by* Lewis Childs

Mons *by* Jack Horsfall and Nigel Cave
Néry *by* Patrick Tackle
Aisne 1914 *by* Jerry Murland
Le Cateau *by* Nigel Cave and Jack Shelden
Walking the Salient *by* Paul Reed
Ypres - **1914 Messines** *by* Jack Sheldon and Nigel Cave
Ypres - **1914 Menin Road** *by* Jack Sheldon and Nigel Cave
Ypres - **1914 Langemark** *by* Jack Sheldon and Nigel Cave
Ypres - **Sanctuary Wood and Hooge** *by* Nigel Cave
Ypres - **Hill 60** *by* Nigel Cave
Ypres - **Messines Ridge** *by* Peter Oldham
Ypres - **Polygon Wood** *by* Nigel Cave
Ypres - **Passchendaele** *by* Nigel Cave
Ypres - **Airfields and Airmen** *by* Mike O'Connor
Ypres - **St Julien** *by* Graham Keech
Ypres - **Boesinghe** *by* Stephen McGreal
Walking the Somme *by* Paul Reed
Somme - **Gommecourt** *by* Nigel Cave
Somme - **Serre** *by* Jack Horsfall & Nigel Cave
Somme - **Beaumont Hamel** *by* Nigel Cave
Somme - **Thiepval** *by* Michael Stedman
Somme - **La Boisselle** *by* Michael Stedman
Somme - **Fricourt** *by* Michael Stedman
Somme - **Carnoy-Montauban** *by* Graham Maddocks
Somme - **Pozières** *by* Graham Keech
Somme - **Courcelette** *by* Paul Reed
Somme - **Boom Ravine** *by* Trevor Pidgeon
Somme - **Mametz Wood** *by* Michael Renshaw
Somme - **Delville Wood** *by* Nigel Cave
Somme - **Advance to Victory (North) 1918** *by* Michael Stedman
Somme - **Flers** *by* Trevor Pidgeon
Somme - **Bazentin Ridge** *by* Edward Hancock
Somme - **Combles** *by* Paul Reed
Somme - **Beaucourt** *by* Michael Renshaw
Somme - **Redan Ridge** *by* Michael Renshaw
Somme - **Hamel** *by* Peter Pedersen
Somme - **Villers-Bretonneux** *by* Peter Pedersen
Airfields and Airmen of the Channel Coast *by* Mike O'Connor
In the Footsteps of the Red Baron *by* Mike O'Connor
Arras - **Airfields and Airmen** *by* Mike O'Connor
Arras - **The Battle for Vimy Ridge** *by* Jack Sheldon & Nigel Cave
Arras - **Vimy Ridge** *by* Nigel Cave
Arras - **Gavrelle** *by* Trevor Tasker and Kyle Tallett
Arras - **Oppy Wood** *by* David Bilton
Arras - **Bullecourt** *by* Graham Keech
Arras - **Monchy le Preux** *by* Colin Fox
Walking Arras *by* Paul Reed
Hindenburg Line *by* Peter Oldham
Hindenburg Line - **Epehy** *by* Bill Mitchinson
Hindenburg Line - **Riqueval** *by* Bill Mitchinson
Hindenburg Line - **Villers-Plouich** *by* Bill Mitchinson
Hindenburg Line - **Cambrai Right Hook** *by* Jack Horsfall & Nigel Cave
Hindenburg Line - **Cambrai Flesquières** *by* Jack Horsfall & Nigel Cave
Hindenburg Line - **Saint Quentin** *by* Helen McPhail and Philip Guest
Hindenburg Line - **Bourlon Wood** *by* Jack Horsfall & Nigel Cave

Cambrai - **Airfields and Airmen** *by* Mike O'Connor
Aubers Ridge *by* Edward Hancock
La Bassée - **Neuve Chapelle** *by* Geoffrey Bridger
Loos - **Hohenzollern Redoubt** *by* Andrew Rawson
Loos - **Hill 70** *by* Andrew Rawson
Fromelles *by* Peter Pedersen
The Battle of the Lys 1918 *by* Phil Tomaselli
Poets at War: Wilfred Owen *by* Helen McPhail and Philip Guest
Poets at War: Edmund Blunden *by* Helen McPhail and Philip Guest
Poets at War: Graves & Sassoon *by* Helen McPhail and Philip Guest
Accrington Pals Trail *by* William Turner
Gallipoli *by* Nigel Steel
Gallipoli - **Gully Ravine** *by* Stephen Chambers
Gallipoli - **Anzac Landing** *by* Stephen Chambers
Gallipoli - **Suvla August Offensive** *by* Stephen Chambers
Gallipoli - **Landings at Helles** *by* Huw & Jill Rodge
Walking the Italian Front *by* Francis Mackay
Italy - **Asiago** *by* Francis Mackay
Verdun: **Fort Douamont** *by* Christina Holstein
Verdun: **Fort Vaux** *by* Christina Holstein
Walking Verdun *by* Christina Holstein
Zeebrugge & Ostend Raids 1918 *by* Stephen McGreal

Germans at Beaumont Hamel *by* Jack Sheldon
Germans at Thiepval *by* Jack Sheldon

SECOND WORLD WAR

Dunkirk *by* Patrick Wilson
Calais *by* Jon Cooksey
Boulogne *by* Jon Cooksey
Saint-Nazaire *by* James Dorrian
Walking D-Day *by* Paul Reed
Atlantic Wall - **Pas de Calais** *by* Paul Williams
Atlantic Wall - **Normandy** *by* Paul Williams
Normandy - **Pegasus Bridge** *by* Carl Shilleto
Normandy - **Merville Battery** *by* Carl Shilleto
Normandy - **Utah Beach** *by* Carl Shilleto
Normandy - **Omaha Beach** *by* Tim Kilvert-Jones
Normandy - **Gold Beach** *by* Christopher Dunphie & Garry Johnson
Normandy - **Gold Beach Jig** *by* Tim Saunders
Normandy - **Juno Beach** *by* Tim Saunders
Normandy - **Sword Beach** *by* Tim Kilvert-Jones
Normandy - **Operation Bluecoat** *by* Ian Daglish
Normandy - **Operation Goodwood** *by* Ian Daglish
Normandy - **Epsom** *by* Tim Saunders
Normandy - **Hill 112** *by* Tim Saunders
Normandy - **Mont Pincon** *by* Eric Hunt
Normandy - **Cherbourg** *by* Andrew Rawson
Normandy - **Commandos & Rangers on D-Day** *by* Tim Saunders
Das Reich – **Drive to Normandy** *by* Philip Vickers
Oradour *by* Philip Beck
Market Garden - **Nijmegen** *by* Tim Saunders
Market Garden - **Hell's Highway** *by* Tim Saunders
Market Garden - **Arnhem, Oosterbeek** *by* Frank Steer
Market Garden - **Arnhem, The Bridge** *by* Frank Steer
Market Garden - **The Island** *by* Tim Saunders
Rhine Crossing – **US 9th Army & 17th US Airborne** *by* Andrew Rawson
British Rhine Crossing – **Operation Varsity** *by* Tim Saunders
British Rhine Crossing – **Operation Plunder** *by* Tim Saunders
Battle of the Bulge – **St Vith** *by* Michael Tolhurst
Battle of the Bulge – **Bastogne** *by* Michael Tolhurst
Channel Islands *by* George Forty
Walcheren *by* Andrew Rawson
Remagen Bridge *by* Andrew Rawson
Cassino *by* Ian Blackwell
Anzio *by* Ian Blackwell
Dieppe *by* Tim Saunders
Fort Eben Emael *by* Tim Saunders
Crete – **The Airborne Invasion** *by* Tim Saunders
Malta *by* Paul Williams
Bruneval Raid *by* Paul Oldfield
Cockleshell Raid *by* Paul Oldfield

Battleground Europe

Airfields and Airmen
Somme

Mike O'Connor

Series editor
Nigel Cave

Pen & Sword
AVIATION

To my mother-in-law Iris (a.k.a The Old Goat, Daft Old Bat, etc)
who, for some strange reason, seems to quite like me.

First published in Great Britain in 2002 by Leo Cooper

Reprinted in 2013 by
PEN & SWORD AVIATION
An imprint of
Pen & Sword Books Ltd
47 Church Street
Barnsley, South Yorkshire
S70 2AS

Copyright © Mike O'Conner, 2002, 2013

ISBN 978 0 85052 864 0

The right of Mike O'Connery to be identified as Author
of this work has been asserted by him in accordance with
the Copyright, Designs and Patents Act 1988.

Printed and bound in England
By CPI Group (UK) Ltd, Croydon, CR0 4YY

Pen & Sword Books Ltd incorporates the Imprints of Aviation, Atlas,
Family History, Fiction, Maritime, Military, Discovery, Politics, History,
Archaeology, Select, Wharncliffe Local History, Wharncliffe True Crime,
Military Classics, Wharncliffe Transport, Leo Cooper, The Praetorian Press,
Remember When, Seaforth Publishing and Frontline Publishing

For a complete list of Pen & Sword titles please contact
PEN & SWORD BOOKS LIMITED
47 Church Street, Barnsley, South Yorkshire, S70 2AS, England
E-mail: enquiries@pen-and-sword.co.uk
Website: www.pen-and-sword.co.uk

CONTENTS

Introduction by Series Editor.. **6**
Acknowledgements.. **8**
Author's Introduction... **9**
Table of Maps.. **13**

How the Guide works.. **12**
The Development of Military Flying.. **14**
An Explanation of German ranks.. **22**
Abbreviations... **23**
The Order of Battle of the RFC 4 Brigade 1 July 1916...................... **24**

Chapter One   **The Northern Area**.. 27
Chapter Two   **The Southern Area**.. **101**
Chapter Three **The Eastern Area**... **148**

Conclusion.. **187**
Further Reading... **187**
Selective Index... **190**

INTRODUCTION BY SERIES EDITOR

I am writing this introduction shortly after visiting an aircraft museum. None of the aircrafts were dated from the Great War, though there were some flimsy looking specimens from the inter war years on display. Looking at these closely, I was again forcibly struck by how delicate these machines looked; I knew I would have had to be paid very good money to fly in the thing in peacetime, let alone in a bitter conflict where the inexperienced airman, the novice to the Western Front, was so vulnerable to those who had become skilled predators. And, of course, their machines were that much more primitive. Certainly the British pilots and observers amongst them operated without parachutes. My mind still continues to boggle at the thought!

I am sure that the bravery of these men is something that draws people to study airmen and their machines in such detail, even from those who have no other particular interest in the Great War. Biographies of airmen exist in disproportion to those of other servicemen from the First World War. For some, especially the Red Baron, there are several, and doubtless there will be several more. People become fascinated by the personality that was able to undertake the extremely hazardous task of engaging in aerial operations.

The area covered by this book encompasses the most visited part of the battlefield by the British and Commonwealth pilgrim or tourist. The Somme battlefield has this great resonance with the British, and its open, rolling fields; small, sleepy, often seemingly deserted villages; occasional dark and foreboding woods; and general absence of the hustle of modern life combine to make it a thought provoking place to go. Whilst the evidence of the fighting on the ground still remains to some limited degree, that of the fighting in the air has almost disappeared. It was a few years ago, whilst on a tour with my father and a friend, that we visited Bertangles and tried to make sense of the location of the airfields there. Not much luck. It was at that time that I thought that it should be possible to adapt the Battleground Europe series to encompass airfields and airmen. It was not just a case of finding airfields; it was also an attempt to put these men, about whom so much has been written, into the context of the villages or chateaux where they were based.

Some years before my visit to Bertangles to seek the airfield, I had come to see the site of von Richthofen's grave. Prior to that I had visited the site where his aircraft crashed, not far from Corbie. At the time I reflected that hundreds more people came to look at a former burial place, unmarked, than came to visit Lieutenant Miller, an American serving in the RFC, who had been in his squadron for twenty-six days. His is the only Commonwealth War Grave in the cemetery.

The fate of downed and killed airmen whose graves have been lost also provokes more than usual interest. Many have been the attempts to pin down the location of the body of Mick Mannock, VC. As I tour the Somme battlefield, turning left at Factory Corner, beyond Flers, heading back to the Albert - Bapaume road, I rarely fail to think of Major Lanoe Hawker, VC, lying out there in a field, in all probability, somewhere to the east, close to the site of Luisenhof Farm.

This book will take visitors to places where they can feel closer to these great men of another age. Mike also covers in this book some of those extraordinarily heroic airmen who manned the observation balloons. One often reads about aircraft shooting these things down in flames, but rarely of the men who crewed and worked from them.

This book will be an invaluable addition to anyone who has the slightest interest in Great War aviation; and for those of us whose interest generally lies more on terra firma it will remove the excuse that we cannot find the airfield, and even when we do we know very little about it in any case. And, as we read the individual stories, it should remind us, too, just how unusual and courageous these men in the sky were.

Nigel Cave
Derrys Wood, Surrey

ACKNOWLEDGEMENTS

I would first of all like to acknowledge the help of Nigel Cave, whom I conspicuously failed to mention in the first volume! His help has been invaluable, not only with proofreading, but with essential ideas for the book layout. Fortunately, he says he is used to ungrateful authors!

Secondly, I would like to thank Jon Wilkinson of Pen and Sword, for his enthusiasm for the series, which has produced, what I think, is a superb layout. He also was omitted from the last acknowledgements, due to taking over the book after the manuscript was completed.

My next thanks have to go to the unprotesting members of *Jasta* 99, Richard Owen, Jim Davies and Peter Holloway. They put up with my requests for proofreading, and translation, and ended up out of pocket. This year we have had three new members posted in to the unit, Nick Kelly, Barry Gray and Dave Leah, whose help has been invaluable.

I would also like to thank the following: Colin Ashford GAvA for his splendid cover illustration; Paul Baillie; the Commonwealth War Graves Commission; Norman Franks; the German War Graves Commission; Hal Giblin; Christine Gregory of the RAF Museum; Trevor Henshaw; Alex Imrie for his assistance with the German side; Phil Jarrett; Wing Commander Jeff Jefford; Stuart Leslie for his great help with photographs; Bob Lynes; Joe Michie; Simon Moody, also of the RAF Museum, for permission to quote from the Brancker and other papers; Mrs Edith Neale; the Newspaper Library; the staff of the *Archive de Picardie*; John Penfold (Pendj): the staff of the Public Record Office; Alex Revell; the staff of the *Service Historique de l'Armée de l'Air* and permission to use the photographs in the Cachy section; Jeff Taylor; the Theatre Museum at Covent Garden; Bruce Robertson; Les Rogers; Ray Sturtivant; the Royal Aeronautical Society for permission to use their certificate photographs held by the RAF Museum; Jean Vilbaj (*Bibliothèque d'Amiens*); Mr A K Williamson-Jones and Barry Woodward.

Every effort has been made to contact the authors of the various books or articles quoted and their copyright is acknowledged.

8

INTRODUCTION

This volume, the second in the *Airfields and Airmen* series, was originally intended to cover the air war from the Amiens - Doullens road, east over the Somme area and then right across beyond Cambrai. However, at a very early stage it was realised that there was far too much information for one volume. After a discussion with the series editor, Nigel Cave, it was decided to split it into two books. The next guide will cover the Cambrai area.

This volume covers the air war from the earliest days until the very last. We have the RFC arriving at Amiens in August 1914; the introduction of the first true fighters with the Fokker *Eindecker* and the De Havilland DH2; and finally the important use of air power in the Allied offensive of August 1918. We also visit, arguably, the two best-known RFC aerodromes on the Western Front, of which one, Vert Galand, is today the most recognisable for the visitor. At both of these sites a number of significant events occurred.

The military background of the Somme area

In July 1915 the expanding British army took over the line north of the River Somme from the French. Number 3 Wing of the RFC, consisting of Nos. 4, 8 and 11 Squadrons, moved down from St Omer to support the Third Army and, in January 1916, III Brigade was formed. Near the end of February 1916 the newly formed Fourth Army took over the line from Gommecourt to Curlu in the south. Another RFC unit, IV Brigade, was formed on 1 April to support the new army and was to be involved in the Battle of the Somme, which commenced on 1 July 1916. (See the RFC Order of Battle for 1 July 1916, on page 24).

The new IV Brigade was commanded by Brigadier-General E B Ashmore, who had handed over his I Brigade to Brigadier-General D le G Pitcher. 'Splash' Ashmore had served in the South African War with the Royal Horse Artillery, where he had been severely wounded. After attending Staff College in 1906 he then held various staff

Brigadier-General Edward Bailey 'Splash' Ashmore, CMG MVO, commanded IV Brigade RFC during the Battle of the Somme in 1916.

9

appointments with the War Office. During this period he gained his Royal Aero Club certificate, No. 281, on 3 September 1912, at the age of 40. In 1917 he was General Officer Commanding the Aerial Defence of London. In the post-war years he founded the Observer Corps and retired in 1929 as a Major-General. During the Second World War he raised and commanded a battalion of the Home Guard and died in 1953.

In early 1917 the British army took over more of the French line, down to the Amiens - Villers Bretonneux road and then, shortly after, still further south to Roye. In order to support this extra frontage IV Brigade was supported by the formation of V Brigade, commanded by Brigadier-General C A H Longcroft.

There was probably more movement of the front line in this area than on any other part of the British sector. This was due to three main reasons. Firstly, during the Battle of the Somme the British army advanced the front line, with tremendous casualties, some five miles. Secondly, in early 1917 the Germans unexpectedly withdrew up to 25 miles to a new defensive line, named by the Allies the Hindenburg Line. Lastly, in their big offensive in the spring of 1918, the Germans made enormous advances and were only just held at Villers-Bretonneux - almost at the gates of Amiens.

This war of movement meant the evacuation of existing aerodromes and retreat to new ones by both sides. A number of aerodromes changed hands twice. For instance, Lechelle was constructed by the British when the Germans retreated to the Hindenburg Line, as the Allied aerodromes were now too far behind the lines. In the German advance of spring 1918 the Bessonneau hangars and Nissen huts were occupied by *Jagdgeschwader* 1, and then in early October 1918 the aerodrome was re-occupied by the RAF during the German retreat.

THE GUIDE

There have been many guides to the various battlefields of the Western Front, some of them extremely detailed, but there have not been any concerning the flying aspect. Using old photographs, maps and contemporary accounts I visited old aerodrome sites and was amazed how little many of them had changed. You can hold up an old photograph of some of them and the scene behind today appears only to lack the aeroplanes. In fact many of the farms associated with these aerodromes have probably changed little in two or three hundred years. For the military historian most of the First World War has a convenient chronological and geographical sequence in that one can relate how far a battle progressed (or not, as the case may be) on a day-by-day basis. The air war unfortunately does not fit into this tidy pattern. Squadrons or flights would take off from one point, have a fight or range an artillery battery at another, and casualties would be spread all over the front, on both sides and many miles behind the actual fighting. Casualties from a single air battle might be buried in different cemeteries miles apart.

This guide has attempted to link interesting events and individuals together, into some sort of logical and digestible order, despite the differences in time and geography. The choice of personalities and events is purely my idea of what is interesting. There has always been the glamour of the scout or fighter pilot and the 'aces' and in recent years there has been what I consider an unhealthy obsession with trying to discover 'who shot down whom'. This at best is a risky past-time, taking into account the confused nature of an air battle, the fallibility of human memory and the marked absence of German records. The air war was not just about aces but involved all the mundane tasks of photography, reconnaissance, artillery ranging, bombing, tank co-operation, infantry co-operation, supply dropping and all the myriad tasks that enabled the Allied armies win the war. To concentrate on just one aspect of the aerial battle does not do justice to the rest.

However, in a book of this kind one cannot ignore the 'aces' theme, though I use the information of 'who got whom' advisedly and would hope that I have presented a reasonably balanced picture of what the first air war was like.

THE COMMONWEALTH WAR GRAVES COMMISSION

The Commission never fails to impress me and any praise for them is too little. They care for my grandfather (and my mother) and maintain the beautiful cemeteries with what seems a ridiculously small workforce. I have trouble keeping my garden under control and yet they maintain acres of manicured grass and lovely flower beds to perfection, with a mere handful of staff.

I would urge all visitors to the cemeteries to record their comments in the Visitors Book, for this not only shows the Commission and its staff that their work is appreciated, but it also keeps alive the memory of the thousands of servicemen buried there.

HOW THE GUIDE WORKS

At the beginning of the guide is a map of the entire area covered by this volume. On it are marked the major towns and the aerodromes, with an overlap so that the reader can also relate places to features that appear in other volumes.

THE TOURS AND DIRECTIONS

The guide has three tours for ease of presentation but there is no compulsion for the visitor to follow these and the reader can visit individual sites at random. Each tour has its own map with the locations of all the points to be visited, plus most of the places that are mentioned in the text. However, if you cannot find a certain point or feature, refer to the first overall map in the book. All maps and aerodrome diagrams are aligned with north at the top. All are to scale but not necessarily the same scale.

There are directions from one site to another. The Somme area is predominantly agricultural and therefore the directions are much simpler than the heavily industrialised area covered in the previous volume in the series, *Airfields and Airmen:Ypres*.

I would strongly suggest that paying a few francs for the yellow Number 52 Michelin 1/200,000 scale map covering the area is a sound investment, particularly the edition that has all the Commonwealth War Graves Cemeteries marked. These maps have a separate insert giving the cemetery location decodes.

AERODROMES

For all aerodrome entries there is an associated plan, with present day buildings annotated. This should enable the reader to orientate himself. Also noted, are the locations of some of the buildings and other features that once stood there. On most plans there are arrows that are aligned with present day photographs, which explain more fully the layout and views you can expect to see. The arrow has a number alongside it referring to the relevant photograph. The exceptions to this are Cachy and part of Cappy in Chapters Two and Three. Insufficient evidence was available to produce detailed plans. Again, because the Somme area is predominantly agricultural, none of the aerodromes we will visit have disappeared under industrialisation, as in the previous volume concerning Ypres.

Many of the points of interest that you can visit were established on farms or near chateaux. They are of interest to you and me but please remember that these are private residences and they do not like hordes of visitors crossing their property any more than you would. Please respect their privacy and use your discretion.

CEMETERIES

In each cemetery entry I have given the Commonwealth War Graves reference number, as it appears on the 1/200,000 Michelin map, so that if you become lost as a result of my directions, you can at least navigate to the relevant location. The reference is given as the map section, followed by the cemetery number. (i.e 9/23 is Couin Military Cemetery, which is cemetery No. 23 in section 9.)

At each cemetery the pertinent grave numbers are given, so that the visitor has a starting point for not only the individual involved but the section of associated text. I would suggest that you view the cemetery register and locate the grave to be visited, as the orientation of some cemeteries can be confusing to start with.

TABLE OF MAPS

1. A Map of the Somme Area
2. A Map of the Northern Tour
3. A Map of the Southern Tour
4. A Map of the Eastern Tour

THE DEVELOPMENT OF MILITARY FLYING

Great Britain

Early Days

Military experiments with balloons began at Woolwich Arsenal in 1878 and a balloon section participated in the Aldershot manoeuvres of 1880 and 1882. These were judged a success with the result that a Balloon Equipment Store was set up at Woolwich by the Royal Engineers to manufacture balloons, instruct in ballooning and serve as a Depot.

In 1883 the Store was transferred to the Royal Engineers Depot at Chatham and was renamed the Balloon School and Factory.

During Sir Charles Warren's expedition to Bechuanaland in 1884 three balloons were employed with a force of two officers and fifteen NCOs and other ranks. After this episode, however, little official interest was displayed and it was only the efforts of a few enlightened officers which kept military ballooning alive. For example, experiments in observing gun fire were carried out, mainly with captive balloons. In 1890 a balloon section was introduced into the army as a part of the Royal Engineers and two years later the centre of balloon work was moved to Aldershot. During the Boer War in 1899 four sections were employed and carried out useful work in directing artillery fire and observation, despite unfavourable conditions and not a little prejudice. In 1905 a better site at South Farnborough was chosen and this evolved into what became the Royal Aircraft Factory (later re-titled the Royal Aircraft Establishment to avoid confusion with the Royal Air Force) and the site of the famous Farnborough air shows. In 1911 the Air Battalion of the Royal Engineers was formed and the Balloon School at Farnborough became No.1 Company and No.2 Company, with aeroplanes, moved to Larkhill in Wiltshire.

The Royal Aircraft Factory

The aeroplane experiments of two aviation pioneers, Lieutenant William Dunne and Mr Samuel Cody, were encouraged by Colonel Capper, superintendent of the balloon factory, despite very meagre financial resources. In September of 1907 the first British army airship, *Nulli Secundus,* flew at the Factory. Cody was involved with this and had been supplying man-carrying kites to the Factory since 1904. The Factory carried out research into all aspects of aeronautics and did much to standardise component parts of aeroplanes. The value of this was demonstrated during the war when a host of furniture and wagon making companies could be subcontracted to manufacture aeroplanes or aeroplane parts. There was criticism from some areas that the Factory was a government monopoly and this came to a head in 1916 with the so-called 'Fokker Scourge' when British losses increased considerably due to obsolete machines. These had been largely products of the Factory. Friction arose as the Factory felt it should supervise and co-ordinate the efforts of the private makers, whilst the independent aeroplane makers feared the paralysing effect of officialdom.

Private enterprise
The British had taken up aviation rather late and were well behind France and Germany. The Royal Aero Club had been formed in 1901 and issued its first Aero Certificate to a qualified pilot, J T C Moore-Brabazon, in March 1910. The first, recognised, powered flight in Britain had been made by Cody in 1908 using a self-built machine, and in 1911 Tom Sopwith had also built his own aircraft, having previously flown mainly French and American designs. He acquired premises at Kingston where, during the First World War, thousands of his aircraft were built, including the legendary Sopwith Camel. There was no shortage of enthusiasm, though most of the early pioneers were reasonably well to do and were spending their own money. By the beginning of the First World War there was a host of aircraft manufacturers, some of them quite small and many destined not to survive the post-war collapse of the aviation industry. Geoffrey De Havilland built his first machine in 1910 but later that year joined the government Royal Aircraft Factory. The main centre for civil aviation was the motor racing circuit at Brooklands where A V Roe had made his inaugaral flight, though there were other centres like Eastchurch, and Claude Graham White's works at Hendon (now the home of the Royal Air Force Museum).

The Creation of the Royal Flying Corps
The lack of official interest and progress in aviation, was continually highlighted by the aviation press, and eventually the government was forced to act. A sub-committee of the Imperial Committee of Defence recommended the creation of a British Aeronautical Service and this came into existence on 13 April 1912. It was called the Royal Flying Corps and was to consist of a Military Wing, a Naval Wing and a Central Flying School. The old No.1

Company became No.1 Squadron and No.2 Company became No. 2 Squadron. In theory it was a combined military and naval air service, but in practice it was doomed to failure with split control. The Naval Wing continued to do its own thing, ultimately becoming the separate Royal Naval Air Service (RNAS).

Between 1912 and the outbreak of war the RFC carried out considerable experimental work in co-operation with the army, aerial photography, bombing, wireless telegraphy and photography.

In the army manoeuvres of 1912 each of the two opposing forces were supplied with an RFC squadron. The defending side was able to use air reconnaissance to locate the attacking force, commanded by General Douglas Haig, whilst the cavalry had been unable to do so - and in a fraction of the time. Grierson, commanding the defending force, used aeroplanes for reconnaissance for the rest of the manoeuvres.

The Royal Naval Air Service

The Royal Navy initially showed interest in airships for the protection of trade routes due to the apparent lack of performance and promise of aeroplanes. After a disastrous start, when their first airship broke its back before even flying, interest quietly lapsed. However, in 1911 a patriotic pioneer pilot, Francis McClean, who owned the site of the flying field at Eastchurch on the Isle of Sheppey, offered to loan two of his machines to train four RN officers. George Cockburn, another pioneer pilot, offered to train them free of charge and Short's provided free technical assistance at their factory. Short Brothers had their factory at Battersea, but later opened another at Eastchurch and became almost the exclusive supplier of seaplanes to the RNAS. Later in 1911 McClean bought another ten acres at Eastchurch and gave it to the Royal Navy to set up their own flying school. Much experimentation was carried out with wireless, seaplanes and flying aeroplanes from ships. Shortly before the war the Navy revived its interest in airships ordering several from different manufacturers, including some from Germany and, in January 1914, airships became the exclusive preserve of the Royal Navy. By the beginning of the war the RNAS had established a number of bases round the coast of Britain.

To War

In June 1914 the RFC concentrated all its squadrons at Netheravon. The mornings were given over to trials and experiments and the afternoons to lectures and discussions. Reconnaissance, photography and moving landing grounds were all practised, and plans for mobilisation were also formulated. Four days were allowed for this, with a move to France on the sixth day.

War came in August 1914. At its declaration No.2 Squadron made the epic flight down from their base at Montrose in Scotland, and yet 2, 3 and 4 Squadrons were all at Dover by the evening of 12 August, with 5 Squadron arriving two days later. 6 Squadron was given the job of preparing the aerodrome at Dover and some of their personnel made up the numbers of the other squadrons. The squadrons crossed the Channel on the morning of 13 August. There had been meticulous planning for this operation with all the support transport collected at Regents Park and consisting of motor cars and commercial vehicles still in the gaudy colour schemes of their previous owners.

The RFC was a tiny force of 276 officers and 1797 other ranks - about half the size of an infantry brigade. It took to the field with virtually all of its available resources and the aeroplanes left behind were largely worn out or scrap. In command of the RFC was Brigadier General David Henderson, who had fought at Khartoum in 1898 and distinguished himself during the Boer War. He had learned to fly at Brooklands at the grand age of 49 and over the next four years was probably the most influential force on the development of British air power.

The four squadrons collected at Maubeuge on 16 August and for two or three days relatively little happened. On Wednesday 18 August the first historic reconnaissance was flown by P B Joubert de La Ferte, in a Bleriot of 3 Squadron and G W Mapplebeck in a BE2 of 4 Squadron. Both became completely lost in cloud but were able to return later, unscathed. The RFC quickly proved its worth and on 22 August large bodies of enemy troops were spotted advancing on the British line. During the retreat from Mons the squadrons moved from field to field, moving in all about ten times in as many days. In particular the RFC spotted von Kluck's attempt to outflank the British Expeditionary Force and the signal was taken personally by Henderson to British Headquarters.

After the Battle of the Marne and the so-called 'Race to the Sea' the RFC moved north with the rest of the British Army and set up headquarters at St Omer, where they soon settled into the pattern that would remain for the rest of the war. With the advent of static trench warfare the style of operation involved mapping enemy trench systems and fortifications, ranging artillery using wireless, photography and bombing. In November 1914 F H Sykes, who was in charge of the RFC at the time, decentralised the RFC and grouped 2 and 3 Squadrons to make 1 Wing, with 5 and 6 Squadrons comprising 2 Wing, each responsible to First and Second Armies respectively.

Expansion

With the massive increase of the British forces on the Western Front there came the last significant change in the RFC structure when, on 30 January 1916, Wings were grouped to make Brigades. A Brigade would consist of a Corps Wing, whose squadrons were dedicated to particular artillery formations in their Army, and an Army Wing with fighter squadrons, whose job was to clear the air of enemy machines and protect the Corps aircraft. By the end of the war a Brigade could have more than two Wings, and as the British army took over more of the line from the French further Brigades were formed to support the newly created Armies. Each was a self-supporting organisation with its own Aircraft Park for issuing new machines, its own Kite Balloon Wing and all the other ancillary units such as ammunition columns, lorry parks etc.

The Royal Air Force

The public outcry about the German air raids on Britain, particularly the daylight aeroplane raids of the summer of 1917, forced the government to completely re-appraise the whole question of the air services. A committee under the great South African statesman Lieutenant General Jan Christian Smuts examined all aspects of air policy and organisation. The main feature was to be the establishment of an independent air service by the amalgamation of the RFC and RNAS into a single force, the Royal Air Force, on 1 April 1918. One of the main driving forces during this process was Lieutenant General Sir David Henderson. There was much grumbling from the independent RNAS concerning the loss of their naval terminology and tradition, but nevertheless it worked and many ex-RNAS officers reached the highest ranks of the RAF.

Germany

Zeppelins and balloons

The German experience in many ways was similar to the British, though they utilised airships, particularly the rigid *Zeppelin* type, to a much greater degree.

In 1884 the Prussian Army set up a detachment to examine the use of balloons and by 1901 this had grown to two Companies. Like the RFC they used spherical balloons both tethered and free, but then moved onto the sausage-shaped kite balloon similar to the observation balloons used in the First World War. Even though most of their efforts were directed at airships, in October 1908 the General Staff set up a technical section to observe various areas, including aviation. The War Ministry, bowing to the suggestions of the General Staff, authorised financial help to the most promising of the private aeroplane constructors. A prize of 40,000 marks was put up in 1908 for the first flight by a German aeroplane and this was won in October of that year at Johannisthal near Berlin.

Aeroplane development

The *Albatros Werke* put an aeroplane and a pilot at the disposal of the military, much the same way as Francis McClean had done with the Royal Navy at Eastchurch, and by March 1911 ten pilots had been trained. As a result of a military commission investigating various types of machines seven were eventually purchased. At the army manoeuvres of 1911 aeroplanes gained valuable experience but the army was still more concerned with balloons. Fortunately for the Germans the Chief of the General Staff, General von Moltke, was a far-sighted officer and in 1912 proposed detailed plans of how the aviation services should be organised. The War Ministry was still concerned, however, that the promise of heavier than air flying could suffer a setback and that the flying services were receiving more attention than they should. However these plans did start to come together in October 1913 when *Oberst von Eberhardt* became the first *Inspekteur der Fliegertruppen* on the formation of the office of *Inspektion der Fliegertruppen* (abbreviated to *Idflieg*) Considerable training and expense went in to the *Fliegertruppe* from this date up to mobilisation on 1 August 1914.

The German air organisation

At the outbreak of war there were thirty three *Feldflieger Abteilungen* (field flying companies) with six machines each, with another ten allocated to the fortress towns of Germany, plus twenty three balloon units and twelve army airships, most of which were unsuitable for operations. Each of the eight German Armies were allocated a balloon unit and one *Feldflieger Abteilung,* with another to each Corps. The airships were kept under the control of Army High Command, but due to a variety of factors their numbers were halved within a month and they were never actually used for reconnaissance in the West. The Army High Command was entitled the *Oberste Heeresleitung,* which was abbreviated to *OHL.*

The German air service, like their RFC counterparts, operated a mixed collection of machines, and not until the middle of 1916 did the two-seater units have an aeroplane with a forward firing gun for the pilot and a ring mounted machine gun for the observer at the back. These were designated C-type machines. In addition the Germans were the first to utilise the fixed machine gun synchronised to fire through the propeller. An aircraft equipped with this feature, the single-seater Fokker monoplane, was able to maintain aerial supremacy from mid 1915 until the Spring of 1916.

By March 1915 the number of *Feldflieger Abteilung* had more than doubled, and specialist units were being developed. The bomber force was eventually amalgamated into *Kampfgeschwader der Obersten Heeresleitung* or *Kagohl* (ie *Ka* of the *OHL*) and five of these units were formed.

The first fighter squadrons

Initially the Fokker monoplanes were allocated to two-seater units in twos or threes but for the Battle of Verdun in 1916 they were reorganised into three *Kommandos.* In August 1916 they became *Jagdstaffeln* (hunting squadrons, abbreviated to *Jastas*). Equipped with the new biplane D-type single-seat machines replacing the out-dated E-type monoplanes, and with a strength of a dozen aeroplanes, these *Jastas* were the first true German fighter units. Finally in October the position of *Kommandierender General der Luftstreitkräfte (Kogenluft)* was created and was now responsible for all German flying units (except the German navy and Bavarian ones) including training and reported directly to the Chief of the General Staff of Armies in the Field. This was the formation of the German Army Air Service.

All flying units were re-organised and the old *Feldflieger Abteilung* became *Flieger Abteilung* and the artillery units were re-designated *Flieger Abteilung* (A). The former carried out long range reconnaissance for army headquarters and the latter the duties of infantry co-operation and artillery observation. Units were no longer responsible to individual Corps but allocated to each Army and as such were very similar to the shape and operation of the British Brigade system that had evolved a few months earlier. The head of each Army's flying units was titled *Kommandeur der Flieger (Kofl)*.

The *Amerikaprogamm*

With the entry of the United States into the war, Germany realised that American industry would soon be a deciding factor and a decision must be forced before this happened. The flying services embarked on a major expansion, which they called the *Amerikaprogramm,* calling for an increase of forty *Jagdstaffeln* and seventeen *Flieger Abteilung* (A), in addition to massive increases in aircraft production and training. In June 1917 *Jastas* were grouped together into *Jagdgeschwader,* when *Jastas* 4, 6, 10 and 11 combined to form *Jagdgeschwader* 1. The target of forty fighter units was achieved, but in practice most were only up to half strength, and in the end the two-seater units increased by only six of the projected seventeen, though the strength of some others was increased.

In March 1918 the German army launched its last great offensive to try and obtain a breakthrough before the might of the American forces could become decisive. The use of new tactics and the new reserves, brought from the Eastern Front, very nearly triumphed. Losses in the *Luftstreitkräfte*, or German Air Service, were high.

The End

In June 1918 *Kogenluft* produced another expansion plan but German industry was unable to meet these targets, due to the lack of raw materials. The training of pilots and observers could also not keep up with demand. Finally, the Allied blockade reduced the amount of fuel that German aeroplanes were able to use. At the Armistice on 11 November 1918, the German army had some 280 flying units and a personnel total of about 4,500, which was considerably less than the RAF. Nevertheless, it had been effective in the way it had been employed.

Under the terms of the Armistice the German air service handed over all its fighters and bombers and though some aeroplanes were used in fighting on the Eastern front during 1919 it was officially disbanded in May 1920.

German ranks and their British equivalent

German army

German	British
Oberst	Colonel
Rittmeister	Cavalry Captain
Hauptmann	Army Captain
Oberleutnant	Lieutenant
Leutnant	Second Lieutenant
Fähnrich	Officer Cadet
Offizierstellvertreter	Warrant Officer
Vizefeldwebel	Sergeant Major
Feldwebel	Sergeant
Unteroffizier	Corporal
Gefreiter	Private (First Class)
Flieger	Private

German navy

German	British
Kapitänleutnant	Captain
Leutnant zur See	Lieutenant
Oberflugmeister	Senior NCO (flying service)
Vizeflugmeister	NCO (flying service)
Flugmeister	Airman (flying service)

Abbreviations

AEO	Assistant Equipment Officer
AFC	Air Force Cross
AFC	Australian Flying Corps
BE	Bleriot Experimental
CB	Companion of the Bath
CBE	Commander of the Order of the British Empire
CMG	Companion of the Order of St Michael and St George
CO	Commanding Officer
CVO	Commander of the Royal Victorian Order
CWGC	Commonwealth War Graves Commission
DCM	Distinguished Conduct Medal
DFC	Distinguished Flying Cross
DFM	Distinguished Flying Medal
DH	De Havilland
DSC	Distinguished Service Cross
DSO	Distinguished Service Order
FA	*Flieger Abteilung*
FA(A)	*Flieger Abteilung (A)*
FE	Farman Experimental
FEA	*Flieger Ersatz Abteilung*
FB	Fighting Biplane
GC	Group Captain
GCB	Knight Grand Cross of the Bath
GCMG	Knight Grand Cross of the Order of St Michael and St George
JG	*Jagdgeschwader*
KB	Kite Balloon
KBE	Knight Commander of the Order of the British Empire
KCB	Knight Commander of the Order of the Bath
KG	Knight of the Order of the Garter
LVG	*Luft-Verkehrs-Gesellschaft*
MC	Military Cross
NCO	Non Commissioned Officer
OC	Officer Commanding
OM	Order of Merit
POW	Prisoner of War
RAF	Royal Air Force
RAS	Reserve Aeroplane Squadron
RE	Reconnaissance Experimental
RFC	Royal Flying Corps
RN	Royal Navy
RNAS	Royal Naval Air Service
SE	Scouting Experimental
USAS	United Stated Air Service
VAD	Voluntary Aid Detachment
VC	Victoria Cross

The RFC Order of Battle
Battle of The Somme 1 July 1916

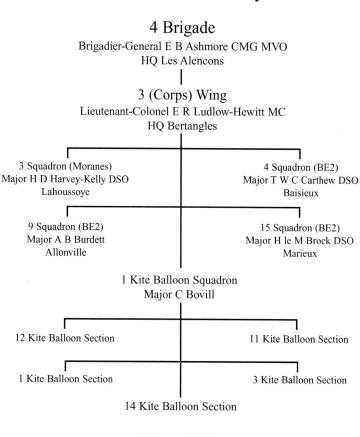

4 Brigade
Brigadier-General E B Ashmore CMG MVO
HQ Les Alencons

3 (Corps) Wing
Lieutenant-Colonel E R Ludlow-Hewitt MC
HQ Bertangles

3 Squadron (Moranes)
Major H D Harvey-Kelly DSO
Lahoussoye

4 Squadron (BE2)
Major T W C Carthew DSO
Baisieux

9 Squadron (BE2)
Major A B Burdett
Allonville

15 Squadron (BE2)
Major H le M Brock DSO
Marieux

1 Kite Balloon Squadron
Major C Bovill

12 Kite Balloon Section

11 Kite Balloon Section

1 Kite Balloon Section

3 Kite Balloon Section

14 Kite Balloon Section

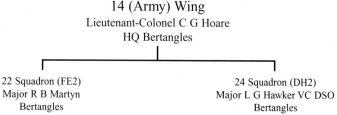

14 (Army) Wing
Lieutenant-Colonel C G Hoare
HQ Bertangles

22 Squadron (FE2)
Major R B Martyn
Bertangles

24 Squadron (DH2)
Major L G Hawker VC DSO
Bertangles

4 Army Aircraft Park
Major A Fletcher
Beauval

24

The Somme Area

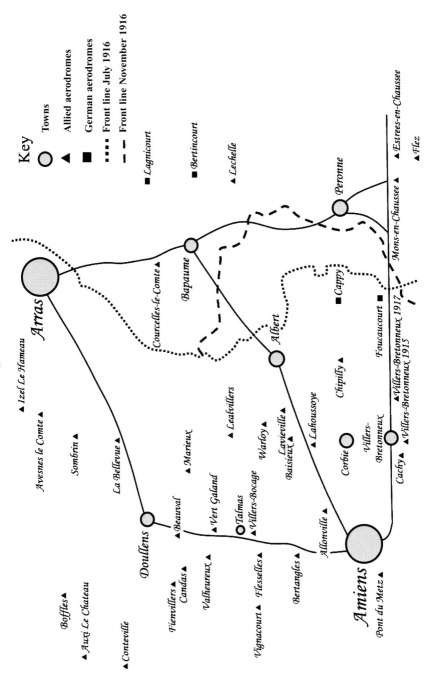

Key

- ⬤ Towns
- ▲ Allied aerodromes
- ■ German aerodromes
- ···· Front line July 1916
- – – Front line November 1916

Boffles ▲

▲ Auxi Le Chateau

▲ Conteville

Avesnes le Comte ▲

Sombrin ▲

▲ Izel Le Hameau

Arras

La Bellevue ▲

Doullens

Fienvillers ▲
Candas ▲

▲ Beauval

Valheureux ▲

▲ Vert Galand

Vignacourt ▲   Flesselles ▲

◯ Talmas

▲ Villers-Bocage

Bertangles ▲

Marieux ▲

▲ Lealvillers

Warloy ▲
Lavieville ▲
Baisieux ▲

Courcelles-le-Comte ▲

Bapaume

Albert

Chipilly ▲

Corbie ◯

Villers-
Bretonneux

▲ Lahoussoye

Allonville ▲

Amiens

Pont du Metz ▲

Cachy ▲   ▲ Villers-Bretonneux 1915

▲ Villers-Bretonneux 1917

Foucaucourt ■

■ Cappy

Peronne

Mons-en-Chaussee ▲

▲ Estrees-en-Chaussee

▲ Fiez

■ Lagnicourt

■ Bertincourt

▲ Lechelle

The Northern Area

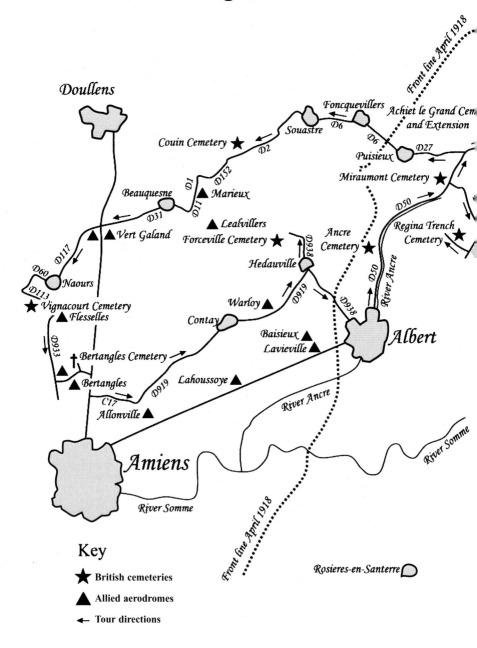

Doullens

Couin Cemetery ★

Souastre

Foncquevillers

Achiet le Grand Cem
and Extension

D6

D6

D27

Puisieux

Miraumont Cemetery ★

D2

D152

D1

D11

Beauquesne

D31

▲ Marieux

▲ Lealvillers

Forceville Cemetery ★

▲ Vert Galand

Hedauville

D938

Ancre
Cemetery ★

D50

Regina Trench
Cemetery ★

River Ancre

D117

D60

D113

Naours

★ Vignacourt Cemetery
▲ Flesselles

Warloy ▲

D919

Contay

Baisieux ▲

Lavieville ▲

D50

D938

Albert

D933

✝ Bertangles Cemetery →

▲ Bertangles

D919

Lahoussoye ▲

C17

Allonville ▲

River Ancre

River Somme

Amiens

River Somme

River Somme

Front line April 1918

Key

★ British cemeteries

▲ Allied aerodromes

← Tour directions

Rosieres-en-Santerre

Front line April 1918

Chapter One

SOMME: THE NORTHERN AREA

This itinerary covers the area from Albert to just west of the Doullens - Amiens road. Most of this area remained in British hands throughout the war, apart from the period after the German offensive of spring 1918 when Albert fell, the advance being halted just to the west of the town. On this tour the places that will be visited, together with the main points of interest, are:

Ancre Military Cemetery - Cedric Lee and 'Those Magnificent Men'
Regina Trench Military Cemetery - a USAS casualty
Miraumont Communal Cemetery - Major V A Barrington-Kennett
Achiet-le-Grand Communal Cemetery - C R Mackenzie, 8 Naval
Achiet-le-Grand Communal Cemetery Extension - 59 Squadron
Couin British Military Cemetery - Basil Hallam, actor, KB Observer
Vert Galand Aerodrome - Albert Ball VC and Harvey-Kelly
Vignacourt Military Cemetery - R J Fitzgerald, an escaped prisoner of war
Bertangles Aerodrome - G S M Insall VC and L G Hawker VC
Bertangles Communal Cemetery - von Richthofen's first burial site
Forceville Communal Cemetery Extension - a victory by L W B Rees VC

From Albert proceed north along the D50 to Hamel. Just beyond the village on the left side of the road is Ancre British Cemetery.

Ancre British Cemetery

This cemetery (9/53) was originally known as Ancre River No. 1 British Cemetery, V Corps Cemetery No. 26, and contained 517 graves, almost all from the 36th and 63rd (Royal Naval) Divisions. After the Armistice seven other smaller cemeteries were concentrated here and, with other battlefield graves as well, there is now a total of 2,500 burials. We are visiting Cedric Lee who is buried in the far left corner of the cemetery from the entrance, near to the Cross of Sacrifice.

Cedric Lee and Those Magnificent Flying Machines (IV A52)
Today aeroplanes and airpower are an accepted fact of life and no

army or navy can operate without aerial superiority. However, in the pre-First World War era the flying machine was a plaything of the rich or well-to-do, without any real practical application. Few could envisage the potential or the enormous effect on the future of warfare the aeroplane was to have.

Most of us have seen and greatly enjoyed the film *Those Magnificent Men in Their Flying Machines*, with its carefree and whimsical atmosphere. Remember the hilarious scene where Count Emilio Ponticelli is shot down by a blunderbuss, when he is accidentally caught in the duel between Count Manfred von Holstein and Pierre Dubois? He and his machine end up in the sewage farm. The aeroplane was a replica of the Lee-Richards Annular biplane - one of the many private designs produced before the Great War.

Cedric Lee was a wealthy engineer and weaver whose father was a partner in the Manchester textile firm of Tootal, Broadhurst, Lee and Co. and his interest in aviation went back as far as 1909. In late 1910 Lee met George Tilghman Richards, formerly a draughtsman with Rolls-Royce, who had set himself up as an independent engineer and designer and Lee invited him to assist as a mechanical engineer. Cedric Lee had bought an Annular Biplane from its designer and builder J G A Kitchen, who had done little with it. During trials Lee and Richards found that the machine refused to leave the ground and eventually Lee turned it over when he ran into a gully. The machine came to an inglorious end when, in late 1911, a gale blew down the hangar where it was being repaired and it was destroyed. Over the next three years Lee and Richards conducted experiments with models and then full-size gliders before building three powered annular monoplanes.

All three were destroyed in non-fatal crashes, though the design in

The original Lee-Richards Annular biplane. The picture is probably taken at Famine Point, on Middleton Sands in Lancashire, where Kitchen kept the machine.

The replica Lee-Richards Annular biplane nearing the end of its restoration by members of the Archive at Shoreham airport in July 2001.

fact proved a success. The last crash involved Lee himself who had minimal flying experience and had never actually qualified as a pilot! The machine climbed at a steep angle and Lee, having lost his nerve, huddled in the cockpit resigning himself to the inevitable crash. The machine fell sideways and crashed inverted into the River Adur, alongside the aerodrome at Shoreham. Despite this, Lee was able to swim ashore unscathed. War had recently been declared and, although he had spent £17,000, Lee abandoned his experiments. Not withstanding his great involvement with aviation he obviously felt his loyalties lay elsewhere and he joined the Royal Naval Division instead. He was killed in action on 13 November 1916, at Beaumont Hamel, serving with the Anson Battalion.

The replica of the Annular Biplane, like the original machine, never actually flew and in the film's flying sequences was suspended from wires. After years of neglect while in storage it is now being restored by members of the Archive at Shoreham airport in Sussex, where the flights of the powered Annular Monoplanes were made. (For further reading see *Aeroplane Monthly* for September and October 1976, where there is an excellent two-part article by Phil Jarrett on Cedric Lee and his aeroplanes entitled *Circles in the Sky*.)

Continue along the D50 towards Miraumont. In the centre of the village turn right at the D107 sign to Courcelette. Proceed past Adanac Cemetery on your left and turn right at the Courcelette sign. Pass through the village and as you leave there is a green Commonwealth War Graves sign on the right to Regina Trench. The narrow metalled road soon becomes a dirt track. The cemetery is on the right.

Regina Trench Cemetery

Regina Trench (9/47) was originally constructed by the Germans. After changing hands a number of times it was eventually cleared by the 4th Canadian Division in November 1916. There are over 2,000 graves and we have come to visit the only American interred here. He is buried about half way down the cemetery, just left of centre.

Lieutenant E D Shaw USAS (IX A9)

Readers may remember that in the previous volume in the series, *Airfields and Airmen: Ypres*, we visited the grave of Lieutenant Gus Kissell USAS at Pont du Hem Military Cemetery. He is probably one of only two United States Air Service casualties that lie under a Commonwealth War Graves Commission headstone.

We shall now visit the second, First Lieutenant Ervin David Shaw, killed with his observer, Sergeant Thomas Walter Smith, both from 48 Squadron RAF. Shaw was the son of Mr and Mrs D C Shaw of 27 Broad Street, Sumter, South Carolina.

9 July was a cloudy day with occasional showers and they left their base at Bertangles at 1800 hours for a reconnaissance. Their Bristol Fighter was shot down in combat with three Pfalz scouts in the Albert area. It seems possible that they were brought down by *Leutnant* Otto Konnecke of *Jasta 5*, as his twenty-second victory. *Jasta 5* were based at Boistrancourt, south-east of Cambrai and Konnecke was one of their most successful pilots, claiming 35 Allied machines and receiving the coveted *Pour le Mérite*. (See *Airfields and Airmen: Cambrai*, Chapter One, Boistrancourt entry.) There are headstones for both Shaw and Smith but they have the same number, suggesting that it is a single

Bristol Fighter A7115 of No. 48 Squadron. The squadron marking of two white bars was discontinued after 22 March 1918. The Bristol Fighter was one of the great designs of the war and soldiered on with the RAF until the 1930s.

grave. On my last visit someone had placed French and American flags on Shaw's grave as US Independence Day had been celebrated a few days before.

This incident highlights one of the problems which historians have in that this is all the information available. The records of RFC/RNAS/RAF squadrons are kept in the Public Record Office at Kew and vary considerably in quantity and quality. Some records were lost, others destroyed and, unfortunately, virtually none of 48 Squadron's records have survived.

Retrace your route back to the centre of Miraumont. As you stop at the main road through the village you will see on the other side of the street the Rue de Cimetière. Continue down this until you come to the cemetery gates. The military plot is in the right hand corner surrounded by a low hedge.

Miraumont Communal Cemetery

Miraumont Communal Cemetery does not have a Commonwealth War Graves Commission number on the Michelin map as it is a civilian burial ground. The military plot is surrounded by a low hornbeam hedge. There are about 30 First World War graves and a small number of Second World War ones. Major V A Barrington-Kennett's grave is on the right in the near corner.

Major V A Barrington-Kennett

Victor Annesley Barrington-Kennett, the third son of Colonel B H Barrington-Kennett of Her Majesty's Bodyguard, was born in June 1888 and had been educated at Ludgrove School, Eton and Balliol College, Oxford. At Oxford he was Captain of the Boat Club and had rowed at Henley. The Barrington-Kennett family suffered terribly in the Great War as, of the four sons, three were killed in action.

Victor's eldest brother Basil had been the Adjutant of the RFC when they went to France in August 1914 but returned to his old regiment and was killed in action. He is buried at Le Touret British Military Cemetery, northeast of Bethune. (See *Airfields and Airmen: Arras.*)His youngest brother, Aubrey, was wounded during the Battle of the Aisne and died in September 1914. He is buried at Vailly British Cemetery, east of Soissons.

Victor's interest in aviation began with ballooning and he later became a second lieutenant in the London Balloon Company, Royal

31

The Barrington-Kennett brothers. Left to right are Godwin, Basil and Victor. At the extreme right is their father. Second from right is a cousin, Guy.

Engineers (Territorial Force). On 5 March 1912, he was awarded his aeroplane Royal Aero Club Certificate, No. 190, and after the London Balloon Company was disbanded in 1913, he transferred to the Royal Flying Corps Special Reserve. Posted to No. 1 Squadron he went with them to France in March 1915, becoming a flight commander before being posted home at the beginning of July. After a spell instructing at No. 2 Reserve Aeroplane Squadron he was posted to 15 RAS as acting commanding officer. In November 1915 he was Mentioned in Despatches and on 24 February 1916, was posted to France to command No. 4 Squadron. Though the unit was a Corps squadron engaged in reconnaissance and artillery observation, certain squadrons were issued with one or two Bristol Scouts to chase off enemy

Bristol Scout 5574. The Bristol Scout was a delightful and popular aeroplane but not really suitable as a fighter.

Max Immelmann in his Fokker *Eindecker*. Note the machine gun synchronised to fire forward through the propeller arc.

aeroplanes. Barrington-Kennett, or 'B-K' as he was affectionately known, flew 4 Squadron's Bristol Scout. Barely three weeks after joining the squadron he had the misfortune to run into Max Immelmann, a much more experienced fighter pilot, and, with the Fokker *Eindecker*, flying a much superior aeroplane.

The Fokker was the first true fighter, as the machine gun was synchronised to fire through the propeller arc. This was superior to RFC machines, which had awkward offset or over wing mountings to avoid the propeller, making aiming difficult.

In Immelmann's biography *Max Immelmann Eagle of Lille*, written by his brother Franz, (who also served in the German Air Service), there appears the following account of the Barrington-Kennett action:

I took off at 12 (noon) in company with another Fokker pilot, Lieutenant Mulzer, to keep order in the air further south. Several minutes later I saw our batteries firing on an enemy airman to the south of Arras. So off I went there. When I arrived, I saw a German biplane and another one about 100 meters above it. As they were doing one another no harm, I thought the second one must be German too. Nevertheless, I flew up and finally spotted the cockades. Now for it, I thought, and fired...peng...peng...peng and then, after a few shots my gun jammed.

I turned away from him, cleared the gun and made another attack. Mulzer had arrived by then, and he joined in. So now we

An

Royal Flying Corps.

Flugzeug mit Major V. B a r r i n g t o n . - K e n n e
ist bei Serre abgesturzt.   Führer tot.

                                    Deutsche Flieger.

The message dropped by the Germans advising the RFC of Barrington-Kennett's death.

concentrated our fire on him. I sent out 700 rounds of ammunition fire, while Mulzer let off 100. Bump! Down he went like a stone into the depths and came to earth at Serre village. Naturally both the inmates were killed and the machine completely wrecked. The remains lay so near the firing line that the English bombarded them with their artillery to prevent us going there. So we were unable to see the results of our work.

Shortly afterwards I had another fight with an English biplane. But unfortunately he got home.

We flew home, feeling pleased with ourselves. I landed first and promptly made my report. Mulzer did not see the machine go down and thought it crashed on English ground. We did not learn

The personnel of *FA*62 on 20 January 1916. In the front row, Oswald Boelcke is fourth from the left and Max Immelmann is second from the right. Both are wearing the *Pour le Mérite* at the neck. In the rear row extreme left is Max Mulzer.

it was on German territory until we rang up to ask. Then I was naturally very happy. No. 10 at last! The double-figures series has started.

Mulzer later served with *Kek Nord* and *FA*32 and after his eighth victory became the first Bavarian airman to be awarded the *Pour le Mérite* or Blue Max. Awarded Bavaria's highest award for bravery, the Knight's Cross of the Military Max-Joseph Order, he became Max Ritter von Mulzer. On 26 September 1916, he was killed in a flying accident: the first Bavarian ace and the first Bavarian fighter pilot to be knighted was dead.

In edition No. 40 of *Stand To!*, the Journal of the Western Front Association, there is an article concerning the Barrington-Kennett brothers by Nigel Wood.

Max Immelmann

Max Immelmann was born in Dresden on 21 September 1890, and in 1905 went to the Dresden Cadet School, becoming an Ensign in 1912. In November 1914 he learned to fly and in March 1915 was posted to *Feldflieger Abteilung* 62 flying LVG two-seaters. This unit, like a number of others, had a few single-seat Fokker *Eindeckers* allocated to them and the more aggressive pilots flew these on escort duties and hunting patrols. The Fokkers became attached units and those of *FA* 62 were designated *Kampfeinsitzer-Kommando (KeK) Douai.* The stars of the new unit were Immelmann and Oswald Boelcke (see *Airfields and Airmen: Ypres* page 136 for more on Boelcke). Immelmann brought down his first official victory on 1 August 1915, and by the end of the year had claimed a total of seven. After his eighth victory he was awarded Prussia's highest award, the *Pour le Mérite*. Both Boelcke and Immelmann became household names in Germany and were showered with awards from the other states in Germany. (For further reading concerning the bewildering number of awards for which fliers were eligible there is a magnificent series of books entitled *Aviation Awards of Imperial Germany* by Neal O'Connor.)

As a Saxon, Max Immelmann is wearing Saxony's most prestigious award, the Military St Henry Order, above the Prussian *Pour le Mérite*.

35

Fokker EIII 210/16 shortly after its capture. It is now in the Science Museum in London.

Immelmann was not to survive long after his downing of Victor Barrington-Kennett. Three months later, on 18 June, and having increased his score to fifteen, he was involved in a fight with FE2bs of 25 Squadron. Captain G R McCubbin and his observer Corporal J H Waller were credited with bringing him down, but the Germans maintained that the machine gun synchronisation gear had malfunctioned, shooting off his propeller. The unbalanced engine then shook the aeroplane apart and the remains fell into the German side of the lines. Immelmann, one of Germany's first popular heroes, was brought back to Dresden for burial. (For more information concerning Immelmann's career, see *Under the Guns of the German Aces*.)

The British were able to evaluate the Fokker and its synchronisation gear when an example fell into their hands on 8 April 1916. It was captured intact when the pilot became lost on a delivery flight from the *Armeeflugpark* at Valenciennes to his aerodrome at Wasquehal, north east of Lille. Today this is the only genuine Fokker EIII remaining and is displayed in the Science Museum in London.

Return to the centre of the village and turn left along the D50 towards Achiet-le-Petit. From Achiet-le-Petit continue along the D9 to Achiet-le Grand. Just before the railway crossing in Achiet-le-Grand turn left at the green Commonwealth War Graves Commission sign. The civilian and military cemeteries are next to each other.

Achiet-le-Grand Communal Cemetery

Proceed to the communal cemetery first, in which there are only three British burials. In the far left corner is the isolated grave of C R Mackenzie RNAS.

The village of Achiet-le-Grand changed hands at least three times during 1917 and 1918 but from April 1917 until March 1918 the 45th and 49th Casualty Clearing Stations were based here and the station was used as a railhead. The communal cemetery and the extension (10/55) were used by both the British and the Germans. Over 600 Allied casualties were concentrated here from the battlefield and approximately twenty German and communal cemeteries in the area.

Colin Roy Mackenzie 8 (Naval) Squadron (3)

Flight Commander Colin Mackenzie DSC, *Croix de Guerre,* **of 8 Naval Squadron, killed 24 January 1917.**

In the autumn of 1916 the RNAS responded to a request to send a squadron down to the Somme to help relieve pressure on the RFC. In order to make up a squadron of eighteen machines a flight of six aeroplanes was taken from each of the three Dunkirk Wings. Number 1 Wing supplied six Sopwith Pups, 5 Wing sent six Sopwith 11/2 Strutters and 4 Wing six Nieuport scouts commanded by Flight Lieutenant C R Mackenzie. The squadron was quickly organised under the able leadership of Squadron Commander Geoffrey Bromet, and most of the unit moved down to Vert Galand on 26 October 1916, for duty with 22 Wing RFC.

In *Naval Eight*, the history of the squadron during the First World War, there is this description of Mackenzie:

A pilot, even though he were a superb flier, did not necessarily become a successful Flight-Commander, and I have known many Flight-Commanders who, by no stretch of the imagination, could be called good pilots, but whose leadership was of a high order.

Initiative, clear sight, navigating ability, the power to impart knowledge and balanced judgement are some of the main attributes which made the successful Flight-Commander in the Great War.

Number 8 Squadron, Royal Naval Air Service, later known as "Naval 8" - a name which was given to it by the Royal Flying Corps pilots of the squadrons with which it worked - and known now in the Royal Air Force as Number 208 Squadron was singularly fortunate in starting its career with several men who were born leaders. To these men many of us owe not only our gratitude, but everything we possess, for, had it not been for their care and foresight, their skill in adapting themselves to strange conditions and their initiative, we would not in our turn have

*been able to lead flights and pass on the knowledge they gave us.
Such a man was Colin Roy Mackenzie, my Flight Commander
when the Squadron went down to work with the Royal Flying
Corps on the Somme front in 1916.*

*At that time we knew little about aerial fighting, for the area
where we had been (Nieuport, Ostend and Dunkirk) was amply
defended by anti-aircraft guns. Unlike some of our Allies, the
Germans believed in manning their anti-aircraft guns with some
of their finest gunners, and I for one certainly take off my hat to
them for their shooting.*

*Our scanty knowledge of aerial fighting was soon augmented
by bitter experience; the enemy were employing a great number
of aeroplanes of every description on this front in 1916, and
Mackenzie led us magnificently through those hectic days when
we hardly knew what we were doing. I remember how he told us
that when we were having a fight with another aeroplane we
must bear in mind that there were two very frightened men in the
picture, but the other man was the more frightened of the two.
What excellent advice! For surely, if one could truly believe this,
a battle was half won before the start. I could write much of these
early days of the squadron, of the escapades we had, of
Mackenzie's warnings to us when we were about to be picked off
by enemy scouts, but I must resist this temptation, or the limited
space at my disposal will be exhausted long before I have
touched on all I wish. The Squadron suffered a great blow when
Mackenzie failed to return one day after an offensive patrol, and
we heard from the enemy, after I had dropped a message over the
lines asking for information, that he had crashed fatally and was
buried with full military honours. So passed a born leader and a
brave man.*

This was praise indeed, as the author of this piece was R J O
Compston, who ended the war as a Major, commanding 40 Squadron
RAF, having claimed some 25 German machines and been awarded the
DSO and DSC with two Bars - one of the Royal Naval Air Service's
great fighter pilots. (The naval Distinguished Service Cross was the
equivalent of the army's Military Cross.)

Colin Mackenzie was born on 3 May 1892, and before service in the
RNAS had been a Surgeon Probationer in the Royal Naval Volunteer
Reserve. He had learned to fly at Eastchurch in August 1915 and had
then been posted to the RNAS' main area of operations at Dunkirk. He
quickly made his mark and received a Mention in Despatches for a raid

on the German aerodrome at Mariakerke and was then awarded a *Croix de Guerre* by the French for shooting down an enemy kite balloon in flames in the face of intense anti-aircraft fire. A further Mention in Despatches was received for his work with 8 Naval while attached to the RFC. His confidential reports in his records are excellent and one of them described him as a *brilliant fighting pilot and Flight Leader*.

On 24 January 1917, Mackenzie left Vert Galand in a Sopwith Pup for an Offensive Patrol and was last seen at midday over Bapaume in pursuit of an enemy machine. He appears to have been the last victim of Hans von Keudell, a founder member of *Jasta 1* before he became commanding officer of *Jasta 27*. Von Keudell was killed only three weeks later on 15 February. (See *Airfields and Airmen: Ypres* page 127.)

Mackenzie's commanding officer, Squadron Commander G R Bromet (later Air Vice-Marshal Sir Geoffrey Bromet KBE, CB, DSO) had this to say of him:

I find it quite impossible to express adequately my admiration for this splendid Officer and great gentleman. In the air, a fine pilot and a brainy and courageous leader who inspired immediate and lasting confidence, and whom the Flight would follow anywhere. On the ground, a keen student of air tactics and fighting methods, a first-class organiser, a loyal and able Officer and the life and soul of any Mess. Small wonder that he was a universal favourite and that we looked upon his loss as irreparable.

Exit the communal cemetery and turn right along the hedge to the military cemetery, where there is the grave of Major Robert Egerton.

Achiet-le-Grand Communal Cemetery Extension

The cemetery has a very attractive entrance consisting of a stone pergola that is covered in wisteria and clematis. In the cemetery there is another pergola and several beautiful mature lime trees. The graves of Robert Egerton and Reginald Benade Glendower Ottley are on the right side of the cemetery adjacent to the Cross of Sacrifice.

The Royal Aircraft Factory Reconnaissance Experimental (RE) 8

The RE8 first flew in June 1916 and was designed to replace the ageing BE2c, the standard two-seater reconnaissance machine employed by the RFC. The initials BE were an abbreviation for Bleriot

RE8 F5892 of 59 Squadron wearing flight markings of 6C. Squadron markings for reconnaissance squadrons were discontinued on 22 March 1918. Note the upper wing extensions, which were prone to failure.

Experimental as Louis Bleriot was considered by the Royal Aircraft factory to be the pioneer of tractor aeroplanes.

Despite a fair amount of criticism of various technical details and the fact it was somewhat heavy on the controls, it was nonetheless a great improvement on the BE2. Unfortunately the RE8 was to receive an undeservedly bad reputation as a result of a number of crashes. In fact the first unit to receive them in November 1916, No. 52 Squadron, exchanged them for BE2s shortly after arriving on the Western Front. (See also *Airfields and Airmen: Cambrai*, Chapter Three, Tincourt New British Cemetery, Major Leonard Parker.) In all sixteen RFC/RAF squadrons would eventually employ the type on the Western Front and it became a useful machine, though it never really shook off the suspect reputation it earned on entry into service.

Major Robert Egerton, CO of 59 Squadron (II C3)

The RE8's reputation was not helped by incidents such as the one involving Major Robert Egerton. He was the son of Sir Reginald Egerton CB and had joined the RFC in early 1915 after service in the Royal Irish Fusiliers. After training at Dover he joined 9 Squadron and went out to France with them on 9 December 1915 but after being wounded in March 1916 returned to England. Egerton was then posted to No. 35 Squadron, which was working up for duty in France and then this unit provided the nucleus for 59

Robert Egerton, commanding officer of 59 Squadron, killed when the outer wing panels of his RE8 collapsed.

40

Egerton in Bristol Scout 4679 of 9 Squadron in early 1916.

Squadron commanders had to sign for everything on assuming command of a unit. This is one of Egerton's successors, Major A P D Hill, taking over 59 Squadron on 27 December 1918.

F.S. FORM 378.

ROYAL AIR FORCE.

CERTIFICATE OF SQUADRON COMMANDERS ON CHANGE OF COMMAND.

(1) Certified that I have taken over Command of No._____**59**_____Squadron. All accounts have been checked with pass books and found correct.

(2) There are no outstanding disallowances by the Paymaster.

(3) The Equipment and Technical Ledgers are correctly kept and the A.E.O. acknowledges his responsibility for deficiencies.

(4) The Conduct Sheets are correct and up-to-date.

(5) The Officers' Mess Accounts are correct; there is a sufficient amount in hand to meet all liabilities. There are no outstanding accounts due from officers.

(6) There are no outstanding accounts against the Squadron for Billeting or against Imprest Account, or of any other description.

(7) I am satisfied with the condition of the Squadron Office, the methods of filing and Register of Correspondence, and that Squadron Records are up-to-date.

Signed_____*A P D Hill*_____
Major RA RAF

Date_____*27. 12. 18*_____191*8*.

Certified that I have handed over command as above.

Signed_____*H. F. Nichols Capt.*_____

Date_____*27. 12. 18.*_____

NOTE.—Changes of A.E.O., etc.

Squadron Commanders must remember that unless they can definitely fix the responsibility for loss or deficiencies upon an individual they themselves are responsible.

(162905) Wt. 15147/1042. 7,000. 7/18. P. & P., Ltd.

Squadron in June 1916. He was appointed acting Commanding Officer of 59 Squadron in August 1916 and led them to France.

Squadron commanders were forbidden to fly on operational sorties, though many chose to ignore this order. Two days before Christmas 1917, Egerton lifted off from 59's aerodrome at Courcelles-le-Comte, about twelve kilometres south of Arras, in RE8 B5095 for a photographic patrol. During a normal dive at 3,000 feet, all four wings outboard of the outermost wing struts failed, though the panels did not completely detach themselves. The aeroplane crashed to earth killing Egerton and his observer Second Lieutenant R B G Ottley. The RE8 was prone to failures of the wing extensions but what makes this crash odd is that the machine had only flown a total of just over nineteen hours. The cause was attributed to the wing main spars being made brittle by frost. Ottley is buried next to Egerton in grave II C4.

Return to Achiet-le-Petit and then follow the D27 to Puisieux. In Puisieux turn right along the D919 for approximately 100 yards before turning left down the D6 to Gommecourt and Foncquevillers. Then follow the signs to Souastre where you then proceed along the D2 to Couin. Just before the village you will see Couin British Cemetery on the left and Couin New British Cemetery on the right.

Couin British Cemetery

The cemetery (9/23) was begun in May 1916 by the Field Ambulances of 48th(South Midland) Division and was used during the Battles of the Somme. It was closed in January 1917 because further extension was impossible. The grave of Basil Hallam (II C15) is towards the far right corner of the cemetery from the Cross of Sacrifice.

Basil Hallam (II C15)

The RFC drew its recruits from all walks of life and here we have a well-known member of the world of entertainment. Hallam was born Basil Hallam Radford, but used only Basil Hallam as his stage name. Born in London in April 1889, he attended Charterhouse before making his professional acting debut in April 1908 at His Majesty's Theatre as Leonardo in *The Merchant of Venice*. During the next six years he

Basil Hallam as a Second Lieutenant, wearing the distinctive maternity jacket of the RFC. He had yet to earn his kite balloon observer's wings.

appeared in a number of plays, in London and New York. It was during his period in New York playing in *The Blindness of Virtue* that he met the actress Elsie Janis, who on her return to England was to appear in the revue *The Passing Show*. Even though Hallam had no experience of revue Elsie Janis suggested that he should try it. *The Passing Show* opened on 20 April 1914, at The Palace Theatre, Shaftesbury Lane and Hallam made an immediate hit with his part of Gilbert the Filbert. He sang three songs during the show, including the hit song Gilbert the Filbert and it ran for a total of 351 performances. His obituary in *The Times* of 24 August 1916, said:

Sheet music for the song *Keep Smiling*, sung by Basil Hallam in the *Passing Show of 1915*. This particular sheet of music was auctioned for $2640 in May 2000.

> ....*the production of the Passing Show at the Palace Theatre in April 1914 established in a single night his position in the first rank of light comedians. Mr. Hallam played the part of a typical prewar "nut" and his song Gilbert the Filbert was soon sung and whistled all over in England.*

His obituary in *The Era* was equally fulsome:

> *His success was instant and complete, and his song Gilbert the Filbert became the rage and the singer the idol of the matinee girl.*

The next year he played in *The Passing Show of 1915*, in which he sang seven songs, but this was less of a success and ran for only 143 performances. Hallam, though a capable dancer, did so with difficulty as he had a steel plate in one leg due to an old injury.

In June 1915 Hallam joined the RFC and was trained at Roehampton for service in kite balloons. Appointed a Balloon Officer in September 1915, he went out to France and joined No1 Kite Balloon Section. On 20 August 1916, he was airborne in high winds when his balloon broke free and, with the prevailing westerly wind, blew him towards the German lines. A witness reported:

> *Hallam was being hauled in and was about 40 yards from the ground when the balloon broke loose owing to the cable snapping. His companion jumped clear and landed safely but Hallam's parachute wouldn't work and he had to stay where he*

A British Drachen type kite balloon employed in 1916. This German design remained in service with the Allies until early 1917, when it was replaced by the superior French Caquot model.

was. One of our planes fired on the balloon as it was drifting fast towards the Hun lines and it began to descend, but Hallam evidently decided to take his chance rather than land in Hunland for he was seen to jump and fall like a log. It is a consolation to know that he must have lost consciousness long before he reached the ground.

It was reported that he was only identified by the silver cigarette case in one of his pockets. The failure rate of parachutes was calculated as one in a thousand jumps and, unfortunately for Basil Hallam, his luck ran out. For the Radford family this was yet another tragedy. Basil's elder brother, Maurice, having been awarded a DSO with the Berkshire Regiment, had been killed in September 1915 and is buried in Vermelles Cemetery, south east of Bethune.

From Couin continue along the D2, which then becomes the D152, to Authie and then the D176 to Thievres. At Thievres turn left onto the D1 to Marieux. South of Marieux the road becomes the D11 or RD 11 depending on which sign you read! At the D31 crossroads turn right to Beauquesne. Continue through the village on the D31 to the D125 crossroads. Here go straight ahead on the D117 for a short distance to the junction of the D25 and Vert Galand Farm.

Vert Galand Aerodrome

This is arguably the most well known British aerodrome on the Western Front, and probably the most recognisable today. The farm buildings, which were alongside the aerodrome, and were used as workshops and Messes, are still in existence and have hardly changed in the last 80 years. It was in continuous use from the summer of 1915 until early 1919 and was home at various times to Nos. 3, 4, 8, 11, 12,

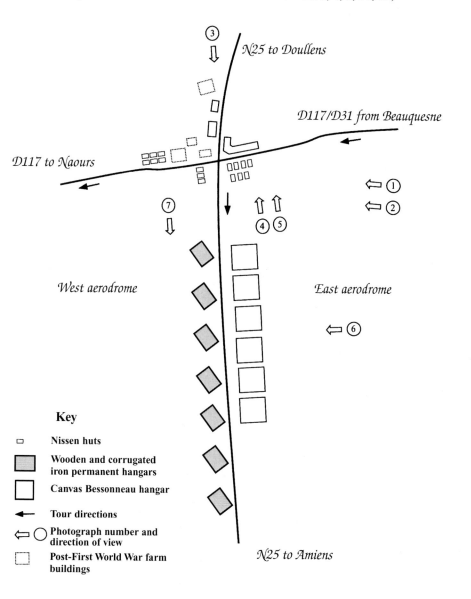

Picture No. 1.Vert Galand in 1918. Permanent hutted camps and ringed by trenches.

Picture No. 2. A similar view taken in July 2001. Though new buildings have been added, the original barns still exist relatively unchanged.

Picture No. 3. Vert Galand Farm in July 2001, looking due south towards Amiens.

13, 15, 19, 22, 23, 32, 56, 57, 59, 60, 66, 70, 84 and 218 Squadrons.

Two very significant events occurred here. It is the aerodrome from which Albert Ball VC, DSO and two Bars, MC, one of the RFC's earliest heroes, and H D Harvey-Kelly, the first RFC pilot to land in France in August 1914, took off on their final flights.

Vert Galand and the Vickers Fighting Biplane (FB) 5

Vert Galand was first occupied in July 1915 with the arrival of 4 and 11 Squadrons RFC. The first Vickers FB5s had been delivered to the RFC in December 1914 and the first machine to go to France, No. 1621, served with 2 and 16 Squadrons, before being captured intact by the Germans at the end of February 1915. They were a great improvement as the observer sat in front of the pilot and had an unobstructed arc of fire, unlike the BE2, where the observer still sat in front but had to fire back over the pilot's head. Number 5 Squadron was the first squadron to have the FB5 in any numbers, but 11 Squadron had the distinction of being the first unit to be wholly equipped with it and also the first to be designated purely for the fighter role.

A J Insall in his autobiography *Observer* (see the bibliography at the end of the book) related what his squadron found when they arrived in

47

Picture No. 4. The DH2s of 32 Squadron at Vert Galand in the summer of 1916. View looking north. The CO, Major T A E Cairnes, is on the right with a walking stick.

Picture No. 5. The same scene taken in 1999.

July 1915:

Officially No. 11 Squadron arrived on the Western Front on 25th July, but the actual transfer from Salisbury Plain to the sloping little field at Vert Galand, to the south of Doullens, on the main road down to Amiens, had taken two or three days. On arrival, we found our senior Flight Commander, Captain L.W.B. Rees, covered in oil and happy as Larry, working like a navvy on his machine, which had already collected a sprinkling of scars from a scrap with an Aviatik or L.V.G. two-seater the day before. He had flown out ahead of the rest of the pilots, in order to make arrangements for the squadron's quarters with No. 4 Squadron, with whom we were to share the 'aerodrome' at Vert Galand pending their removal to Baizieux, down near Albert. (See also the Forceville British Military Cemetery entry later in this chapter for an action involving Rees.)

Insall continues his description of the problems they had in making Vert Galand useable:

When we came to it in 1915 it was sown with lush clover, and the whole Squadron had to fall in and march, and counter-march, and march again, before it became really flat enough for a Vickers Fighter, with two up and all its warlike impedimenta to attempt to unstick from and then clear the line of trees at the far side, with any reasonable margin to spare.

The difficulty was, of course, to find suitable landing-grounds in the immediate proximity to equally suitable farm buildings.

Picture No. 6. Vert Galand on 3 May 1918, looking almost due west. The farm is out of picture to the right. On the other side of the road are the RE8s of 15 Squadron and on this side the RE8s of 59 Squadron.

> The establishment authorised for a Royal Flying Corps squadron
> was 138 other ranks (and nineteen officers), which is quite a lot
> of square-footage when one comes to think about it in terms of
> farms and their outhouses. And one did not just evict the farmers
> and their stock just like that, and hope for the best. Selecting a
> suitable landing-ground was a complicated exercise.

Initially living conditions were fairly primitive, but as Insall further recounted:

> At Vert Galand (unaccountably 'Ladies' Man', for those who
> prefer the Anglo-Saxon) we managed to provide for everyone,
> although it is true that I and one other officer had to make do
> with bell-tents all through our sojourn there, in an orchard
> belonging to the Ferme du Rosel, the farm on the east side of the
> Amiens-Doullens road where our B Flight had its mess. Bitterly
> cold as it was in that tent during the later months of the year, I
> thoroughly enjoyed my tenancy of it, and so I believe did my
> brother stoic, Captain (as he then was) 'Pip' Playfair, R.A., the
> Officer Commanding B Flight, who had his tent alongside mine.
>
> We succeeded in borrowing a couple of rather dubious
> mattresses from the farmer's wife, and I evolved a technique of
> my own that gave me a form of central heating. It was very
> simple, and consisted of the various items of my daytime clothing
> spread one upon the other above the blanket-cloth lining of my
> Service valise, surmounted by my long-tailed leather flying coat.
> By careful infiltration I was able to feed myself into the sleeping-
> bag without disturbing what lay above, and by the time I had
> arrived at my destination my circulation had become more than
> just restored, and I never suffered from frost-bite. And in the
> mornings I would rise to find my clothing pleasantly warm.

'Pip' Playfair had a distinguished career and retired from the RAF in 1942 as Air Marshal Sir Patrick Playfair KBE, CB, CVO, MC. He died in 1974. Insall later became one of the co-founders of the Imperial War Museum in London and after service during the Second World War joined the Shell Petroleum Company's Research Department.

Expansion of Vert Galand

Initially the RFC only occupied the area east of the Amiens-Doullens road but, as with so many aerodromes, it expanded and spread to the western side of the road.

In his wonderful autobiography, *Sopwith Scout 7309*, Patrick Gordon Taylor describes an incident concerning the west aerodrome:

A war artist's dramatic impression of Vickers FB5 1642 of 5 Squadron being shot down in flames by anti-aircraft fire on 20 June 1915. Surprisingly, Second Lieutenants W H D Acland and R V de Halpert survived, though both were injured

Picture No. 7. The Sopwith Pups of A Flight 66 Squadron at Vert Galand in May 1917

Our squadron was located on the west side of the road, where a small area of grassland sloped gently down to a fold in the ground. It was very small, but anybody in doubt about getting into it could land on the big field across the road and taxi back. The snag was that 43, 56 and 19 Squadrons were all based on this big field, and it soon became known that there was some loss of face involved in having to land on the other side of the road. On one occasion this led to a pilot preferring to overshoot, so that he ended up on one of the hangars. Of all people, the pilot was Andrews, and his handling of this potentially shaming situation was so superb that his already very high stock among the pilots went up even more. Caught without engine on his final approach to land, and trying with considerable skill to retrieve the situation, he literally landed on top of the canvas hangar. There was a strong wind at the time and this, coupled with the very low landing speed of the Pup, allowed the aeroplane to subside gently into the folds of the hangar. In due course Andrews emerged from his machine and climbed unhurried to the

Captain J O Andrews, A Flight Commander 66 Squadron, in fug boots and leather flying coat. He retired from the RAF in 1945 as an Air Vice-Marshal with the CB, DSO and MC. He died in May 1989.

52

Andrews in his Sopwith Pup B1703. Note the flight commander's pennants on the rear wing struts.

billowing ground. He stood for a moment, taking off his gloves as if to remove any soiling effects of the incident. Then he turned to the somewhat shaken onlookers and raised his eyebrows slightly: 'Ah, Flight Sergeant Ramsay, there you are. You might have this mess cleared up, please.'

Andrews was commander of A Flight in 66 Squadron and had already completed a tour of duty with Lanoe Hawker's 24 Squadron, where he had been awarded a Military Cross. We shall meet him again later in the chapter in the entry concerning the aerodrome at Bertangles.

Albert Ball VC

Each British Army had its own self contained dedicated RFC Brigade, providing all the air support necessary. However, there was one organisation that was directly under the command of Headquarters RFC in the Field. This was 9 Headquarters Wing, which was moved around to bolster any brigade that needed reinforcement during an offensive its army was conducting. It was used in much the same way as von Richthofen's *Jagdgeschwader* 1 was employed by the German High Command. In April 1917, 9 Wing was commanded by Lieutenant Colonel C L N Newall (later Marshal of the Royal Air Force Lord Newall GCB, GCMG, OM, CBE) and comprised seven squadrons. Numbers 27, 55, 57 and 70 Squadrons were based at Fienvillers, together with the Wing Headquarters and 19, 56 and 66 Squadrons were based at Vert Galand.

Number 56 Squadron had been the first to equip with the new Royal Aircraft Factory SE5. Designed around the excellent Hispano-Suiza engine it first flew on 22 November 1916, and the next day was flown by Captain Albert Ball. His initial impressions were not favourable as the stationary-engined SE5 was not as manoeuvrable as the rotary-engined Nieuport. He was granted the privilege of having a Nieuport Scout as well as his SE5 when 56 Squadron moved to France. Ball by this stage was a national hero, having claimed 31 enemy machines by the end of September 1916, flying Nieuport Scouts with 11 and 60 Squadrons. His courage and aggressive spirit had been rewarded with a Military Cross and the Distinguished Service Order with two Bars - the first man to achieve the distinction of three DSOs. The British avoided publicising its heroes, unlike Germany and France where they were lionised and their faces appeared in newspapers and on post cards. However, Ball's return from France at the end of 1916 was given wide publicity and he was feted wherever he went. In February he was made an Honorary Freeman of his home city, Nottingham, but despite all the adulation Ball wanted to return to France. He was appointed commander of 56 Squadron's A flight at London Colney, where they were working up to take the new SE5 to war.

The squadron went to France on 7 April 1917, but were grounded for two weeks whilst various modifications were made to their machines. The first patrol led by Albert Ball was flown on 22 April, though initially they were not allowed to cross the front line. Over the next two weeks Ball was to claim another thirteen German aeroplanes.

In the evening of 7 May 1917, Albert Ball led 56 Squadron out of Vert Galand for the last time. In his superb autobiography *Sagittarius Rising,* Cecil Lewis, a fellow member of 56 Squadron described the patrol:

> *The squadron sets out eleven strong on the evening patrol.*
> *Eleven chocolate-coloured, lean, noisy bullets, lifting, swaying,*

Captain Albert Ball VC in his SE5 A4850 of 56 Squadron at London Colney, prior to moving to France. This is the machine in which he was killed.

turning, rising into formation-two fours and a three-circling and climbing away steadily towards the lines. They are off to deal with Richthofen and his circus of Red Albatrosses.

The May evening is heavy with threatening masses of cumulus cloud, majestic skyscrapes, solid-looking as snow mountains, fraught with caves and valleys, rifts and ravines - strange and secret pathways in the chartless continents of the sky.

Steadily the body of scouts rises higher and higher, threading its way between the cloud precipices. Sometimes, below, the streets of a village, the corner of a wood, a few dark figures moving, glides into view like a slide into a lantern and then is hidden again.

A red light curls up from the leader's cockpit and falls away. Action! He has seen, and they see soon, six scouts three thousand feet below. Black crosses! It seems interminable till the eleven come within diving distance. At last the leader sways sideways, as a signal that each should take his man, and suddenly drops.

Machines fall scattering, the earth races up, the enemy patrol, startled, wheels and breaks.

But the squadron plunging into action had not seen, far off, approaching from the east, the rescue flight of Red Albatrosses patrolling above the body of machines on which they had dived, to guard their tails and second them in the battle. The British scouts, engaging and disengaging like flies circling at midday in a summer room, soon find the newcomers upon them. Then as if attracted by some mysterious power, as vultures will draw to a corpse in the desert, other bodies of machines swoop down from the peaks of the cloud mountains. More enemy scouts, and, by good fortune, a flight of Naval Triplanes.

But, nevertheless, the enemy, double in number, greater in power and fighting with skill and courage, gradually overpower the British, whose machines scatter, driven down beneath the scarlet German fighters.

Ball failed to return and, near the endurance of his machine, was observed to come out of low cloud, inverted and crash near Annouellin, some fifteen kilometres northeast of Lens on the German side of the lines.

Cecil Lewis again:

Of the eleven scouts that went out that evening, the 7th of May, only five of us returned to the aerodrome.

The Mess was very quiet that night. The Adjutant remained in

his office, hoping against hope to have news of the six missing
pilots, and, later news did come through that two had been
forced down, shot in the engine, and that two others had been
wounded. But Ball never returned. All next day a feeling of
depression hung over the squadron. We mooned about the sheds,
still hoping for news. The day after that hope was given up.

Towards the end of May official notification was received from the Germans that Ball had been killed and on 8 June it was announced that he had been awarded a posthumous Victoria Cross.

Albert Ball caught the imagination of the public with his courage, and he epitomised the individuality and fighting spirit of the RFC. The chivalry of the air and his stirring deeds were a bright light after the drudgery of trench warfare and lengthening casualty lists. No odds were too great and his actions inspired a whole generation of fliers. His loss was a great blow, not only to the RFC, but also to the country as a whole.

(For further details of Ball's life see the Annouellin German Cemetery entry in Chapter One of *Airfields and Airmen: Arras*.)

Hubert Dunsterville Harvey-Kelly

Only a little more than a week before Albert Ball was posted missing the RFC had suffered another grievous loss. One of the other 9 Wing squadrons sharing the east field at Vert Galand was No. 19, flying the French Spad fighter and commanded by Major H D Harvey-Kelly DSO.

Harvey-Kelly had been a member of the small band of RFC personnel who crossed the Channel with the BEF in August 1914 and when he arrived in Amiens on the morning of 13 August had the distinction of being the first RFC pilot to land in France. One of the members of 2 Squadron in early 1915 was Sholto Douglas (later Marshal of the Royal Air Force Lord Douglas of Kirtleside GCB, MC, DFC) who recorded his impressions of Harvey-Kelly in his autobiography, Years of Combat:

But the outstanding pilot in the squadron was undoubtedly
H.D. Harvey-Kelly. With fair hair topping a rubicund
complexion, he was one of the most likeable of men, and he was
already famous for his great sense of humour and his
lighthearted and gay approach towards everything that he ever
did. Even in the zestful company of the Flying Corps he was a
noted individualist.

On 29 April 1917, General Hugh Trenchard and his trusty aide

Major H D Harvey-Kelly (right) in front of a 19 Squadron Spad.

Maurice Baring were conducting one of their visits to RFC squadrons, as Baring related in his autobiography *Flying Corps Headquarters 1914-1918*:

> We went to Vert Galand to see Harvey-Kelly, who commands No. 19 Squadron. When we got there we were told he had gone up by himself and one other pilot for a short patrol. We stayed there all the morning. By luncheon time he had not come back. He was due and overdue. When we went away the General said "Tell Harvey-Kelly I was sorry to miss him", but I knew quite well from the sound of his voice he did not expect this message would ever be delivered. Nor did I.

Spad B6802 of 19 Squadron. The aeroplane was rugged and well liked, though only two RFC squadrons, Nos.19 and 23, were fully equipped with it.

59 Squadron was based at Vert Galand from April to September 1918. Here Captain C E Williamson-Jones, B Flight Commander, has the rare pleasure of flying home on leave on 4 June 1918. The machine is an RE8 with the flight marking of 5B.

> *Harvey-Kelly never came back. He was the gayest of all gay pilots.*

April 1917 was a dreadful month for the RFC, with over 300 aircrew becoming casualties and it subsequently became known as 'Bloody April'. The British flying services had survived the Fokker Scourge of the year before by introducing new types such as the DH2 and FE2.

Ground crew were the backbone of the RFC. The fitters and riggers of A Flight 59 Squadron, with pet rabbits.

Another unit based at Vert Galand was 15 Squadron, who were here from April to September 1918. RE8 B6661 '8' with (left to right) 1 A/M Skinner, 1 A/M Grey, Lieutenant L J Derrick and Lieutenant J W Schofield. Derrick was killed the day after the photograph was taken and is buried at Querrieu British Cemetery.

But they were no longer a match for the German Albatros D types, introduced in the autumn of 1916. Newer machines like the SE5 and Bristol Fighter were just coming into service but not in sufficient numbers. The commencement of the Battle of Arras on 7 April 1917, found the RFC at a great technical disadvantage, which could only be countered by aggressive action against the numerically smaller German Air Service.

Harvey-Kelly had only commanded 19 Squadron since 2 February. Three Spads were lost on this day, and it would seem that Harvey-Kelly fell victim to *Leutnant* Kurt Wolff of *Jasta* 11.

See the Amiens Aerodrome section in the next chapter, and for more details of Harvey-Kelly's life see *Airfields and Airmen; Arras,* Chapter One, Brown's Copse Military Cemetery.

Proceed west on the D117 to Naours and from there take the D60 to Wargnies and Havernas. At Havernas join the D933 in a north westerly direction for 100 yards and then at a minor crossroads turn left into Rue de Vert Près to Vignacourt. Continue through the village until you see the left turn indicated by the green Vignacourt Cemetery sign.

Vignacourt Military Cemetery

This area was well behind the front line for most of the war and between October 1915 and March 1918 there were only six burials in the communal cemetery. In March 1918 and the German offensive the front moved much closer, and two Casualty Clearing Stations, the 20th and 61st, were based here. The cemetery (8/10) was open from April until August 1918 and now contains over 600 casualties, including the six original burials.

From June 1918 until February 1919 the RAF had an aerodrome near here where Nos. 8, 15, 20, 29, 54, 80 and 151 Squadrons were based at various times. It was from Vignacourt on 10 August 1918, that Captain F M F West of 8 Squadron took off with his observer, Lieutenant J A G Haslam, for a tank co-operation patrol. During the operation West was severely wounded in a fight with several enemy machines but despite this he returned and passed his valuable information before being removed to hospital. While in hospital in London, having had a leg amputated, he was notified of the award of a Victoria Cross.

The cemetery contains over thirty fliers and they represent the squadrons based in the area who were involved in the bitter fighting of the German advance of early 1918 and their retreat in August of the same year. A quarter of these casualties belonged to No. 3 Squadron Australian Flying Corps who were operating their RE8s from Poulainville and Villers-Bocage. (The AFC had remained independent after the amalgamation of the Royal Flying Corps and Royal Naval Air Service to form the Royal Air Force.) The second largest group served with 65 Squadron at Bertangles, flying the legendary Sopwith Camel.

The cemetery is unusual if not unique in that it contains a monument erected by the village to honour the British dead. It is on the west side of the plot opposite the Stone of Remembrance and was unveiled in August 1921. The statue is of a French soldier and on the base are engraved the words: *Frères D'armes de L'Armée Britannique, tombés au Champ D'Honneur, dormez en paix. Nous veillons sur vous* and is translated thus: "Brothers in arms of the British Army, fallen on the field of honour, sleep in peace; we are watching over you."

All the graves here are of interest but there are a number that are particularly noteworthy. Proceed to the right side of the cemetery where you will find R J Fitzgerald.

Roy James Fitzgerald (II E2)

Fitzgerald's entry in the cemetery register contains the intriguing statement that he was an escaped prisoner of war. He came from Wellington on the southern tip of North Island, New Zealand and at age 27 was slightly older than his contemporaries. Not only was he older but, was also married. Joining the Gloucestershire Regiment in September 1915 he was commissioned shortly after. In 1916 he had been awarded an MC as a temporary second lieutenant, when he was the last remaining unwounded officer from four assaulting companies. He immediately took command, consolidating the defences of the captured position and then led parties to establish posts in an outlying wood. On 8 May 1917, he was captured whilst serving with the 12th Battalion.

R J Fitzgerald, an escaped prisoner of war.

During his internment he met an RFC prisoner of war Geoffrey Harding, who had been shot down while serving with 25 Squadron. Harding's book, *Escape Fever,* is one of the classic escape books of the First War and in it he relates his and Fitzgerald's escape. They met at Ströhen, where the deputy commandant was Karl Niemeyer, later in charge of the notorious Holzminden camp. The continual war between inmates and the Germans was not without its hilarious moments as Harding described:

An early cause of friction arose from the authorities insisting on reading out their orders in German. Very few of us understood the language, yet those who failed to comply with them were punished. Those who did understand did not approve of acting as unpaid interpreters of unwelcome red tape. We therefore insisted on an official interpreter being appointed and pressed the camp staff to accept the onus of ensuring that the orders were understood.

We won our first point and several German aspirants for the post were tried out on parade. Their efforts, for the most part, were lamentable and the strange distortion of our language received such overwhelming applause that Hauptmann Niemeyer, in charge of the parade, determined, one day, to undertake the task himself. Accordingly, he carefully read the orders out in German and then attempted a translation at sight - a most unwise venture. He soon learnt better. He started off fairly well, although he amused us by introducing the phrase, "I guess you know" at the end of each sentence - he had, strangely enough, spent some time in the United States. Just when he appeared to be going to get through the ordeal with comparative credit, he made some incredible error which drew forth much laughter and applause. Had he been a wise man he would himself have passed it off with a laugh, but, instead of doing so, he made the fatal mistake of losing his temper and, in his rage, he gave birth to a winner.

"You tink I know notinks," he yelled, "but I know damn all!"

He left the parade ground hurriedly with hoots of derision ringing in his ears. An efficient interpreter was produced within twenty-four hours.

After Niemeyer departed for Holzminden the situation deteriorated to such an extent that the prisoners went on strike and refused to write home, cash cheques or spend money in the commandant's canteen. The silence from Ströhen became obvious to the authorities at home and a neutral ambassador was appointed to visit the camp. The whole place was thoroughly cleaned, with every stone whitewashed. The ambassador arrived accompanied by a German General and his staff. Harding again related the event:

The General not only went round the camp with the Ambassador but extended the inspection to ourselves. As we had much at stake, we all arranged to behave like good boys; that is, all but Fitzgerald, who decided that the time was ripe for a little personal propaganda.

The "Big Noise" made a careful inspection of the parade and all went smoothly until, almost at the end of his labours, he caught a glimpse of naked flesh. He stopped short, the better to survey the apparition. There in the cold light of day stood Fitzgerald, naked except for an abbreviated pair of under-drawers.

Pandemonium replaced order. The General demanded explanations from the Commandant; awkward explanations. Fitzgerald was required to elucidate the problem of his nudity. He did so, and proved conclusively that the garment he wore was the sole survivor of his wardrobe, which had been pruned progressively during a prolonged sojourn in hospital.

In the absence of satisfactory evidence for the prosecution, no disciplinary action could be taken against Fitzgerald. On the other hand, not many days elapsed before a new Commandant was placed in charge of us.

Harding was intent on escaping from the moment of capture but was unable to have as a partner his pilot, Lieutenant Gerald French, who was left behind at Karlsruhe camp due to the burns he had received when they were shot down. An earlier escapee from Ströhen had been Gilbert Insall VC, who had reached Holland in August 1917. (See the Bertangles section later in this chapter.)

I needed a partner to work with me. I had heard of too many cases of escapes going wrong for want of a comrade and was anxious to pick my man carefully. Curiously enough, the first man I met when a fresh batch of prisoners arrived at Ströhen, was Fitzgerald, a New Zealander, who had been with me in the same division in France, before I joined the RFC. He had come to the divisional school while I was instructing there and had struck me as a level-headed, fearless fellow of fine physique. We had struck up a friendship then and we were now delighted to find ourselves in the same prison camp.

We had a yarn together immediately he arrived and exchanged experiences connected with our capture. He had been severely wounded and had been in hospital a long time. Before twenty-four hours had elapsed I asked him if he would join me in an effort to escape, and we finished by entering into a compact to get away together as soon as possible.

After a couple of abortive attempts to escape they realised that in the other ranks compound next-door two soldiers were allowed just outside the gate each evening in order to fill water containers. Altering their uniforms, they had the agreement of the soldiers involved to take their place and were able to cut the wire between the compounds and mingle with the other occupants. They successfully passed through the gate and as the sentry's attention wandered they dropped their water containers and ran. There were loud whistles as the guards raised the alarm but they were unable to shoot as there was a building obscuring the line of fire. Walking by night and laying up during the day Harding and Fitzgerald walked towards the Dutch frontier. Their food soon ran out and they were forced to steal apples and root vegetables from fields. The biggest discomfort was lack of water, forcing them to drink from puddles and on one occasion purloin milk from churns, the richness almost making them sick.

Conditions became steadily worse and heavy rainstorms added to their misery. On one occasion as they trudged along a railway track a howling gale concealed the noise of an approaching train and they narrowly escaped being run down. They had to swim the wide River Ems and Harding lost his boots, which were strung round his neck by the laces. He then had to march in stockinged feet, which rapidly became swollen bloody lumps. Their luck held, and on the night of 5/6 October 1917, their seventh night on the run, they crossed into neutral Holland.

After some time in a camp, the British Embassy at the Hague obtained passage to England and they arrived in Gravesend at the end of October. While staying at the Waldorf Hotel in London they were besieged by the Press anxious for a good story. A week of interviews with all kinds of staff and intelligence followed, but the highlight of their return was a private audience with His Majesty King George V at Buckingham Palace.

In March 1918 Fitzgerald, who had received a Mention in Despatches for valuable services while in captivity, joined the RFC. After observer and gunnery training he was posted to No. 35 Squadron at Flesselles on 28 May 1918. The unit was equipped with the Armstrong Whitworth FK8 or 'Big Ack', as it was better known in the RFC, though they also had one or two Bristol Fighters for long range artillery ranging. (The letters FK indicate that the designer of the 'Big Ack' was Frederick Koolhoven, a Dutchman).

It was on one of these operations that Fitzgerald was killed. He and his pilot, Lieutenant Allan McGregor, were ranging heavy artillery on ammunition dumps and railway sidings southeast of Cappy, over 17,000 yards behind the enemy lines. The target was hit and so great was the explosion, that smoke reached 3,000 feet and pieces of shrapnel up to 6,000 feet. The total destruction of the dump, sidings

Bristol Fighter B1134 of 35 Squadron, showing the unit marking of a horizontal white line.

and trains was confirmed by photographs taken later. Just as they were finishing the shoot their Bristol Fighter was attacked by ten enemy scouts and in the ensuing fight Fitzgerald was killed in the air and McGregor seriously wounded, though he managed to land on the British side of the lines.

It is surprising that Fitzgerald was allowed to return to France, as the possibility of being captured for a second time would have resulted in him being given a rough time from his German captors in the search for details of his escape. It was a sad end having come half way round the world to fight and then, after being seriously wounded, escape from captivity. You would have thought he had done enough.

Another 35 Squadron crew (IV B4 and IV B5)
There are two further members from 35 Squadron buried in the cemetery and they in many ways epitomise the problems with flying training in the First World War. Of the 9,000 plus personnel killed or died in the British flying services a surprisingly high 37% occurred in the UK. Apart from UK training accidents, many were killed after arriving at operational squadrons due to their inexperience. Flying a heavily loaded warplane was considerably different from a light, unarmed, training machine. Aerodromes on the Western Front were smaller, rougher and frequently less than ideally located. The experience levels of crews joining squadrons was pitiful, many arriving with a mere handful of hours, never having fired a gun or even having flown at night. Once having passed the initial dangerous stage and gained some experience, the chance of surviving a tour of duty increased dramatically.

Second Lieutenants James Gitsham and Leonard Wadsworth departed Flesselles, just four kilometres east of Vignacourt Cemetery,

Armstrong Whitworth FK8 or 'Big Ack' B201 of 35 Squadron.

The original grave markers for James Gitsham and Leonard Wadsworth.

on 29 June 1918, in their heavily loaded 'Big Ack'. Shortly after take off they stalled in a climbing turn and spun into the ground. The bombs exploded, setting the machine on fire and totally burning out the wreckage. Both men were killed. Gitsham had only been in the squadron a month and Wadsworth barely three weeks. Gitsham had come all the way from Australia and had a brother flying with 144 Squadron in Palestine. Wadsworth, who was just a week past his nineteenth birthday, had been a costings clerk before joining up. Their operational career was snuffed out before it had barely begun.

Major Charles Dawson Booker (V C6)

We have come to this grave to pay our respects to one of the great RNAS scout pilots and a brilliant exponent of the Sopwith Triplane. C D Booker was born on 21 April 1897, and resided in Australia until 1911, when he returned to England with his parents.

He joined the RNAS on 18 September 1915, and after training at Chingford and Redcar was posted to 5 Wing. As a result of an attack on the German aerodrome at St Denis Westrem in September 1916 he was Mentioned in Despatches. In late October 1916 he was posted to 8 Naval Squadron, where he was to fly Sopwith Pups initially, though they shortly re-equipped with the Sopwith Triplane. His Triplane, N5482, was named Maud and he was to claim over a dozen German

66

machines in this aeroplane. The Triplane was a classic and much respected by the enemy for its rate of climb. It was in response to the Sopwith that the Germans built their own triplane, the Fokker Dr1.

In May 1917 Booker received the French *Croix de Guerre* and the Distinguished Service Cross, in addition to promotion to flight commander. On 11 August 1917, during an evening patrol, he and W L Jordan became involved in a dogfight over No Man's Land with a black Albatros, which he shot down Unfortunately his machine was damaged by another Albatros and he was forced to land just on the British side of the lines. The pilot of the black Albatros was *Hauptmann* Adolf Ritter von Tutschek commander of *Jasta* 12, who had been awarded the *Pour le Mérite* only a week before. Von Tutschek was badly wounded in the shoulder, though he was later able to resume command of *Jasta* 12.

C D Booker wearing the ribbons of his DSC and *Croix de Guerre*.

On 27 September 1917, Booker scored his twenty-third and last victory before leaving 8 Naval Squadron, his first in a Camel. Together with J H Thompson of 8 Naval and J H Tudhope of 40 Squadron RFC, they caught an Albatros just after it had shot down a balloon in flames and forced the German machine to land on the Allied side of the lines. The pilot, *Oberleutnant* Hans Waldhausen of *Jasta* 37, was captured. The following month Booker was posted back to the UK for a rest.

Sopwith Camels of 201 Squadron. The second machine from the left had a long career. It also served with 209 Squadron, where it was flown by W R 'Wop' May, who narrowly escaped being shot down by von Richthofen on 21 April 1918. It was during this engagement the Red Baron was killed.

In March 1918 he returned to France to command 1 Naval Squadron, shortly before the Royal Air Force was formed on 1 April 1918, with the amalgamation of the RFC and the RNAS. Number 1 (N) Squadron now became No. 201 Squadron RAF. Despite the fact he was not supposed to fly on patrols Booker did, nevertheless. He was to claim another three enemy machines before his death in action on 13 August 1918.

Apart from patrols and showing new pilots the lines, most of which were annotated in the squadron records as 'special missions', he also carried out a lot of test flights. It was on one of these 'special missions', that he was to lose his life. New pilots were a danger to themselves and to the Flight they were with until they had gained enough knowledge to be a useful member of a patrol. By taking new pilots out to instruct them in the procedures to be used and to accustom them to the area in which they were to operate, Booker took a lot of the work and strain off his flight commanders.

The squadron had moved aerodromes a number of times since Booker had taken command but on 13 August they were based at Poulainville (part of Bertangles aerodrome). That morning, on another of his 'special missions' he took a new pilot, Second Lieutenant G H Fowles, for his first look at the lines. What should have been a safe tour around 201's part of the front turned into disaster when they ran into a very large number of Fokkers west of Rosières. In the ensuing fight Fowles kept his head, put his machine into a spin and avoided becoming a casualty, though he returned with his Camel well shot about. Booker, whose actions had undoubtedly allowed his young pilot to escape, was shot down and killed, probably by *Leutnant* Neckel of *Jasta* 19. According to other sources Booker would seem to have shot down three German machines during the fight. Though he claimed nearly thirty enemy machines, making him one of the RNAS' most successful fighter pilots, it seems strange that he never received a DSO or even a Bar to his DSC.

Fowles, a schoolteacher from north Wales, survived the war and was demobilised in September 1919. Neckel received the penultimate German Air Service *Pour le Mérite*; he died of tuberculosis in 1928.

From the cemetery back track to the village centre and turn right onto the D49 until joining the D113 signposted to Flesselles. Continue through Flesselles on the D933. Approximately six kilometres south turn left on the D97 which is signposted to Bertangles. After a short distance you will cross a railway line. Stop here, as this is the centre of Bertangles aerodrome.

Bertangles Aerodrome

This site is probably the next best-known RFC aerodrome on the Western Front after Vert Galand. Used constantly between October 1915 and February 1919 the following squadrons were based here at various times: Nos. 3, 6, 9, 11, 18, 21, 22, 23, 24, 48, 52, 54, 65, 82, 84, 85 and 209.

This entry is by necessity very large as more significant events occurred here than on any other RFC/RAF aerodrome. In fact to make it easier to follow it is worth listing them chronologically:

7 November 1915, G S M Insall of 11 Squadron won his VC flying from here

14 December 1915, G S M Insall became a PoW whilst based here

10 February 1916, The first single seat dedicated RFC fighter squadron, No.24, arrived here

2 April 1916, No. 24 Squadron scored the first RFC single-seat fighter victory

23 November 1916, Major Lanoe Hawker VC, took off from here for his last flight

21 April 1918, 209 Squadron took off from here to engage von Richthofen on his last flight

21 April 1918, Von Richthofen's body was brought here

22 April 1918, Von Richthofen was initially buried in the village cemetery

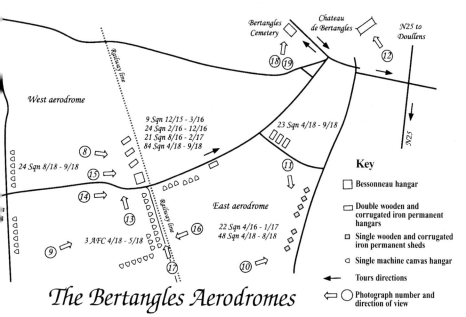

The Bertangles Aerodromes

Picture No. 8. The view to the southeast, looking across the east aerodrome at Bertangles village.

Bertangles, like most aerodromes, is difficult to document due to the lack of specific records and was in effect two aerodromes which straddled the railway line to the southwest of the village. On one side was the West aerodrome and on the other side the East aerodrome. With the German advance in the spring of 1918 many squadrons evacuated their aerodromes and Bertangles became very crowded. Tented hangars were erected around the other sides of the existing fields. Also about this time the confusing designation of Poulainville came into use for one part of the aerodrome. Geographically the south

Picture No. 9.The view to the northeast in July 2001.

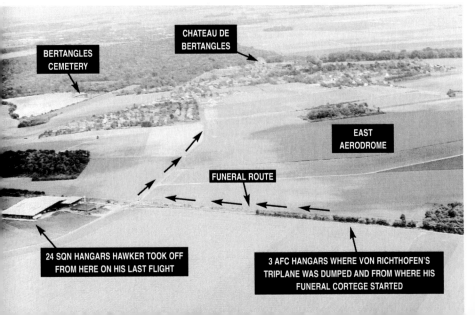

BERTANGLES CEMETERY

CHATEAU DE BERTANGLES

EAST AERODROME

FUNERAL ROUTE

24 SQN HANGARS HAWKER TOOK OFF FROM HERE ON HIS LAST FLIGHT

3 AFC HANGARS WHERE VON RICHTHOFEN'S TRIPLANE WAS DUMPED AND FROM WHERE HIS FUNERAL CORTEGE STARTED

Picture No.10 View of the east field, looking northeast, with the Bristol Fighters of 48 Squadron.

side of the West aerodrome is closer to Poulainville than Bertangles but, without further evidence or documentation, it has proved impossible to establish exactly where this name referred to. In fact, in the past it had been thought that Poulainville was a completely different aerodrome altogether, instead of consisting of one part of Bertangles.

Picture No. 11. The east field again viewed almost due south showing, probably, the FE2s of 22 Squadron. These hangars were destroyed in the German bombing of 24 August 1918.

Picture No. 12. The Chateau de Bertangles, the Mess for the headquarters of both 3 and 14 Wings RFC.

The chateau in the village housed the Messes for the headquarters of both Three (Corps) Wing and Fourteen (Army) Wing RFC, who comprised Four Brigade, though the offices were down in the village. Later the chateau was also the headquarters of Lieutenant General Sir John Monash, commanding the Australian Corps.

Gilbert Stuart Martin Insall VC

Number 11 Squadron arrived at Bertangles in October 1915, having previously been based at Vert Galand and while they were here one of their members received his country's supreme gallantry award.

Gilbert Insall was born in Paris in 1894 and was the eldest son of a dental surgeon. His younger brother was Algernon John Insall, later the author of *Observer*, the book from which quotations are taken at the beginning of the Vert Galand section earlier in this chapter. Gilbert entered Paris University, intending to follow in his father's footsteps but the declaration of war intervened and in September 1914 he joined the Royal Fusiliers. Both brothers were interested in aviation and were accepted into the RFC within two days of each other in March 1915. They had learned to fly earlier in March and Gilbert had gained his Royal Aero Club certificate, No.1110, on 14 March. Algernon obtained his certificate two days earlier and it was numbered 1109. Both brothers then

Second Lieutenant Gilbert Insall VC MC.

A captured Vickers FB5 of 11 Squadron. Note how small and precarious is the observer's front cockpit.

proceeded to Netheravon for further training but Algernon suffered a crash during landing and was off flying for ten days. On his return to flying he discovered he was confident in the air but had completely lost his nerve when it came to landing. Both brothers were scheduled to proceed to France very shortly with No.11 Squadron, which was working up for service overseas, and with little time left Algernon was able to re-muster as an observer.

Number 11 Squadron moved to France at the end of July 1915. They were equipped throughout with the Vickers FB5, which was unusual in that most squadrons of this era still operated a motley collection of types. Also they were intended for 'fighting duties', as opposed to reconnaissance or artillery observation, and thus can be considered as the RFC's first fighter squadron.

Though intended for fighting duties, inevitably 11 Squadron undertook other work such as photographic reconnaissance and on one such operation Gilbert, together with his observer, First Class Air Mechanic T H Donald, drove off two German LVG two-seaters. Over the next few weeks Insall showed a great offensive spirit, attacking a number of enemy machines and this culminated in an epic incident on 7 November 1915. Algernon Insall described the episode in *Observer* thus:

> *As they were about to cross the lines at a height of between 7,000 and 8,000 feet my brother sighted one of the enemy's kite-balloons operating behind the German front, and flew downhill towards it, diving when close enough to attacking order to drop an incendiary bomb upon it - the electrically fired bomb provided in the Vickers Fighter for this type of target.*

Unfortunately, being masked from his objective by a part of his own machine, Gilbert found himself out of line by the time the balloon had come within range, and he had no alternative but to abandon the attempt. An anti-aircraft battery close to the balloon winch opened fire on the Vickers with a form of rocket and my brother was able to pin-point the battery's position before turning away. As he started climbing to gain height, he then observed an enemy two-seater approaching from the north, flying down the line of trenches at some 2,000 feet higher than the Vickers, so he turned back towards the lines, to a position whence Donald was able to use his Lee Enfield. The hostile machine thereupon turned in towards the east while the Vickers Fighter, still gaining height, proceeded to give the impression that it was not intending to press the attack home.

The ruse was successful, the enemy observing that my brother appeared to be disinclined to penetrate further into the German side of the lines, and turning back to follow him. Gilbert allowed the enemy to approach until within range, and then swung his machine around abruptly. As the Vickers came out of the turn, Donald brought the Lewis gun into action. The German machine immediately banked over and dived away, heading for the rocket battery, whether intentionally or not is difficult to say, for in an engagement of this kind such a considered manoeuvre might not readily enter a contestants head.

At all events, Gilbert, as he told me later, saw a chance of 'cutting the fellow off' and took it at once, putting the Vickers into an all-out power dive. Both machines were now travelling at something well above their normal diving-speed, but neither let up, and Donald, taking very careful aim, fired an entire drum (forty-seven rounds) at the enemy two-seater, and had the satisfaction of seeing its engine stop. At this stage both pursued and pursuer entered cloud. Up to that moment the enemy observer had been returning Donald's fire from his machine gun, firing over the tail of his machine, but when the Vickers emerged from the cloud layer the Germans were seen coming heavily to earth in a ploughed field.

Both occupants were observed leaving the machine, one carrying its machine gun, and Donald reopened fire upon them as they started running for shelter, one lagging behind as though injured.

My brother now turned and dived at the stranded machine,

Donald releasing the fire-bomb they had earlier intended using against the kite-balloon. The bomb duly ignited and fell burning, and as the Vickers left the German machine was seen to be enveloped in smoke.

By now troops in a neighbouring village had started firing at the British machine, and things were getting hot for my brother and Donald. Climbing as steeply as possible without sacrificing too much speed, the Vickers started to run the gauntlet of intense fire directed against it from every available machine-gun, and anti-aircraft gun in the vicinity, making for the German reserve trench-line. Here, Gilbert put his nose down and headed for the British side of the line, his machine under increased fire as it approached the German forward positions, round after round striking the Vicker's wings and framework. Finally, a bullet found its mark on the fuel-tank just as the Vickers swept over no-mans-land. The engine at once stopped, and the machine sank to the ground. My brother was just able to clear a small wood near the village of Agny, to the south of Arras, and made a safe landing behind it, a few hundred yards behind the Allied front-line trenches, which at this point were held by the French.

Despite the smoke the German machine, flown by *Offizierstellvertreter* Hoffman and *Leutnant* Mielck of *Fliegerabteilung* 32, was not actually destroyed.

The Germans shelled the Vickers without causing further damage and that night a party from Bertangles replaced the fuel tank and erected canvas screens to hide the machine from German observation. The machine was later moved and French troops were put to work filling shell holes to enable a take off to be made. Eventually, with a sandbag in the front cockpit replacing Donald, Insall took off without any warming of his engine, to the applause of hundreds of French troops, who had gathered to watch his departure. A J Insall again:

When he took off on his way home he took care to show himself to the enemy in their front-line trenches and they acknowledged this piece of effrontery with a wholesale fusillade of machine-gun fire. All his onlookers had had to throw themselves flat on the ground as he took off, because of the hail of bullets that came cracking through the trees.

The citation for the Victoria Cross (the fifth aviation award), which appeared in the London Gazette on 23 December 1915, read thus:

For most conspicuous bravery, skill and determination on 7th November, 1915 in France.

He was patrolling in a Vickers Fighting Machine, with First Class Air Mechanic T. H. Donald as gunner, when a German machine was sighted, pursued, and attacked near Achiet.

The German pilot led the Vickers machine over a rocket battery, but with great skill Lieutenant Insall dived and got to close range, when Donald fired a drum of cartridges into the German machine, stopping its engine. The German pilot then dived through a cloud, followed by Lieutenant Insall. Fire was again opened, and the German machine was brought down heavily in a ploughed field 4 miles south- east of Arras.

On seeing the Germans scramble out of their machine and prepare to fire, Lieutenant Insall dived to 500 feet, thus enabling Donald to open heavy fire on them. The Germans then fled, one helping the other, who was apparently wounded. Other Germans then commenced heavy fire, but in spite of this, Lieutenant Insall turned again, and an incendiary bomb was dropped on the German machine, which was last seen wreathed in smoke.

Lieutenant Insall then headed west in order to get back over the German trenches, but as he was at only 2,000 feet altitude he dived across them for greater speed, Donald firing into the trenches as he passed over. The German fire, however, damaged the petrol tank, and, with great coolness, Lieutenant Insall landed under cover of a wood 500 yards inside our lines. The Germans fired some 150 shells at our machine on the ground, but without causing material damage. Much damage had been caused by rifle fire, but during the night it was repaired behind screened lights, and at dawn Lieutenant Insall flew his machine home with First Class Air Mechanic T.H.Donald as a passenger.

Just over a month later Insall and Donald failed to return from a patrol. They had attacked an enemy two-seater and after being hit the engine had stopped. Both were wounded - Insall by a piece of anti-aircraft shell. In addition to the VC awarded to Insall, Donald received a thoroughly deserved DCM. After two unsuccessful escape attempts Insall was third time lucky and he, together with two companions, reached neutral Holland. For his persistent escape attempts he was awarded a Military Cross. On his return to England Insall received his Victoria Cross from His Majesty King George V at Buckingham Palace on 26 September 1917. After the war he remained in the RAF and retired as a Group Captain in 1945. He died on 17 February 1972. Donald, Insall's companion in the VC action died in 1945.

24 Squadron and the DH2

Number 24 Squadron was formed at Hounslow on 1 September 1916, from a cadre of 17 Squadron. It consisted of one officer, four NCOs and 80 men and the first commander was Captain A G Moore MC and Bar. The squadron's role was training students for service in France, and to complete the establishment of squadrons about to go overseas. This was standard practice for the air services, which were expanding dramatically. In fact, just before 24 Squadron departed for the Western Front they provided the nucleus of 27 Squadron RFC. Another task was training their own instructors for night flying, using Avro 504s, so that they could train other pilots for anti-Zeppelin work for the defence of London. They were responsible as well for the maintenance and manning of the night flying aerodromes at Wimbledon, Sutton's Farm (Hornchurch) and Hainault Farm.

The 24 Squadron crest.
Motto: In Omnia Parati
(Prepared for All Things)

At the end of September 1915 Moore was replaced as commanding officer by Major Lanoe Hawker, who found that he had no flight commanders and that only one machine was serviceable out of the six on charge. With hard work and long hours Hawker was able to bring the squadron up to a fine state of efficiency. In December more personnel arrived, including two experienced officers, Captain R E A W Hughes-Chamberlain and Second Lieutenant J O Andrews, who were to go to France with the squadron.

The unit had operated a mixed collection of machines up to 10 January 1916 until the first De Havilland DH2s arrived at Hounslow. More of the diminutive pushers were delivered and by the end of the month they had a full complement. Little time was available for training and familiarisation for, on 7 February, 24 Squadron flew to France. The crossing of the cold and uninviting Channel was completed safely, despite the fears raised by the unreliability of the 100hp Gnome Monosoupape engine. Of the twelve DH2s which departed Hounslow, ten arrived safely at St Omer, though one ended up on its nose on landing.

The first single seat fighter victory in the RFC

Much was expected of 24 Squadron as the RFC's first single seat dedicated fighter unit. Only two days after their arrival they carried out the first line patrol and unfortunately also suffered their first casualty, the C Flight Commander, Second Lieutenant A E C Archer, who spun into the ground whilst landing at St Omer. No reason could be found for the accident but it was generally considered that Archer had probably lost control as a result of his legs being numbed by the cold. The cockpit of the DH2 was bitterly cold - there was no warm engine to huddle behind and virtually no windscreen to deflect the icy blast of the slipstream. Archer is buried in Longuenesse (St Omer) Souvenir Cemetery.

Hawker was well known for his inventive mind and one of his many ideas was the design of thick boots to keep out the intense cold. He approached Harrods, the well-known Knightsbridge department store, which produced a number of pairs of his sheepskin thigh boots. Given the nickname 'Fug Boots' by the pilots, they were very popular and eventually became officially adopted by the RFC.

On 10 February, 24 Squadron moved to Bertangles but, due to bad weather, with machines force landing en route, they were unable to concentrate there until ten days later. The poor weather, plus a number of technical problems with the machines, meant little operational flying was possible in March.

SHELL DAMAGE

Tidmarsh in front of his DH2, wearing his fug boots. He narrowly escaped death or severe injury when a shell passed through his cockpit while flying at 10,000 feet. Note the damaged nacelle.

However, their luck changed on 2 April when Second Lieutenants S J Sibley and D M Tidmarsh were engaged on a dawn patrol.

Sibley spotted a two-seater Albatros just south of Baisieux at 9,000 feet. He followed it and just north of Albert fired half a drum of ammunition from his Lewis gun into it, upon which it started to dive. Tidmarsh who was flying at 12,000 feet over Bucquoy saw the Albatros

78

Date and Hour	Wind Direction and Velocity	Machine Type and No.	Passenger	Time	Height	Course	Remarks
Total time flown since Sept 4				1915	75 hrs	5 min	
1st April	·	5948	–	1hr50	11000 ft	Army Patrol.	Saw Albatros fired down over Albert. etc.
2nd April	·	5944	–	1hr30	10000 ft	H. A. Patrol.	No H.A. observed
3rd April	·	5944	–	1hr50	10000 ft	Army Patrol.	–
4th April	·	5962	–	10 min	3000 ft	Test flight.	Cleared double feed jam in air.
5th April	–	5952	–	20 min	6000 ft	Test flight.	
6th April	·	5962	–	55 min	10000 ft	Army Patrol.	
7th April	·	5962	–	10 min	5000 ft	Test flight.	machine right wing down.
8th April	·	5962	–	1hr50	12000 ft	Army Patrol.	
9th April	·	5762	1hr10		11000 ft	Army Patrol.	Clouds at 3000 ft.
			Time for week 9 hrs 10 min				

The laconic entry in Sibley's logbook regarding the first RFC single seat aerial victory: *Saw Albatros fired drum over Albert. etc.*

being attacked by Sibley and used the advantage of his extra height to dive after it. From a range of 100 yards Tidmarsh fired a short burst into the German machine before his gun jammed. Both DH2s followed the steeply diving Albatros, whose observer was keeping a steady stream of fire directed at the British scouts. Clearing the jam, Tidmarsh fired off the rest of his drum of ammunition before having to turn for home due to his low fuel state. Sibley last saw the enemy machine in a steep dive at only 1,000 feet over Miraumont. Upon their return to Bertangles the squadron office telephoned the local anti-aircraft batteries who confirmed that an enemy machine had come down between Grandcourt and the River Ancre. The victory was credited to Sibley and Tidmarsh - the first by an RFC single-seat fighter.

Sibley served in 24 Squadron until the end of August when a crash brought his tour of duty to an end. Despite the severity of the crash it did have its humorous side as Sibley later recounted:

My last patrol with the squadron was on 25th August 1916, and after having a scrap with an LVG, I was returning home at about 5 thousand feet, when almost halfway between the aerodrome and the lines I heard a tremendous report - the whole machine started to vibrate to such an extent that the gun mounting broke loose, the undercarriage came adrift - this happened in about one second before I could switch off. I then looked round and found the left hand tail-boom cut through and waving about. I managed to calm down and while doing so, I threw out the Lewis gun which had smashed off the mounting and was across my knees. I crashed in a corn field about 4 miles from another aerodrome, and after crawling out of the wreck, two Frenchmen ran up, who had been working in the field. One gave me something to drink and being light-headed I started to walk to the aerodrome - being guided by a church spire which I kept as a land mark. The day was hot, I was covered in blood from a cut over my eye which I received when the gun mounting came adrift in the air and I gradually took off my clothes, so that when I arrived at Allonville I had only a shirt and my flying hat.

I went into the mess and they - seeing that something was wrong by my lack of clothes- one officer took me back by car to my squadron. Upon arriving being still light-headed I went into the mess to mix myself a drink when in came Hawker. I must have looked a nasty sight. He came over to me at once and enquired what had happened and then took me straight to his hut, where he bathed my head himself and dressed the wound, but as he thought it needed further attending to he took me himself in his car to hospital in Amiens where I had several stitches put in.

Strange to say I could not remember where I had crashed, so patrols had to go out and find the remains of the machine. Hawker told me afterwards, how lucky I was to get away with it. He said the machine was one of the worst wrecks he had seen, and it was afterwards decided that the LVG had put a burst into the engine as several other bullets were found in it, and apparently that was the cause of the cylinder coming out.

S J Sibley (right) with his head bandaged, after his crash on 25 August 1916.

Tidmarsh finished his period with 24 Squadron in October 1916 and returned to the UK. Ironically, both Tidmarsh and Sibley were to become prisoners of war, when flight commanders with 48 Squadron flying Bristol Fighters. They were repatriated in December 1918. Tidmarsh, from Limerick in Ireland, died at an early age in 1944. Sibley having survived two world wars, died as the result of a motorcycle accident at the age of 67 in 1965.

Lanoe Hawker VC

We last met Lanoe Hawker at Abeele where he was serving in 6 Squadron RFC and had been awarded the first Victoria Cross for aerial combat. (See *Airfields and Airmen: Ypres* page 49.)

By September 1915 Hawker had served in 6 Squadron for nearly a year and was badly in need of a rest. His squadron commander, Major Gordon Shephard, was loath to let him go but recommended him for command of a squadron in England. Shephard was later Brigadier General G S Shephard DSO MC, and the highest ranking RFC/RAF officer to be killed in the war. (See *Airfields and Airmen; Arras*, Chapter Two, Lapugnoy Military Cemetery.) On 20 September Hawker returned to Home Establishment. His ability as a leader was recognised by his appointment to command No. 24 Squadron - the RFC's first single seat scout unit. Not only was he building a new squadron but, with his unit being designated for Fighting Duties, he also had to formulate the tactics and training for a new mode of warfare.

During the spring and summer of 1916 the DH2s of 24 Squadron helped defeat the Fokker monoplane and

Major Lanoe Hawker VC, killed in action on 23 November 1916. He has no known grave and is commemorated on the Air Forces Memorial to the Missing at Arras.

DH2 5998 of A Flight, 24 Squadron in front of the sheds at Bertangles. This machine was flown regularly by Captain J O Andrews.

Picture No. 13. The west aerodrome looking northwest along the railway line. These were the hangars used by 24 Squadron in 1916, the middle one was destroyed in the German bombing raid of 24 August 1918. This is also where Lanoe Hawker took off on his last flight.

ended the so-called 'Fokker Scourge'. However, in the early autumn the pendulum was beginning to swing in the Germans' favour again. The first Albatros DI and DIIs were coming into service, faster and equipped with twin machine guns synchronised to fire through the propeller arc. In addition the new machines were being concentrated into *Jagdstaffeln* or hunting squadrons, instead of machines attached to two-seater squadrons.

Hawker, like other commanding officers, was officially forbidden to fly patrols over the lines but this was an unacceptable restriction to Lanoe. He had been advised that shortly he would be promoted to command a Wing but, on the afternoon of 23 November 1916, he accompanied a three-man patrol led by Captain J O Andrews. (In 1917 Andrews was a flight commander in 66 Squadron and we met him earlier in the chapter at Vert Galand.) The other members of the patrol

Picture No. 14. The cross roads photographed in 1999. The 24 Squadron aerodrome is to the left. Bertangles village is in the distance. The wood behind the car is the centre of the east aerodrome.

were Lieutenant R H M S Saundby and Lieutenant J H Crutch, though the latter soon dropped out due to engine trouble. Northeast of Bapaume Andrews spotted two German two-seaters and led the patrol down on them, but they dived away east. Andrews then saw two formations of enemy machines above and was about to turn away when Major Hawker dived past in pursuit of the two-seaters. Obliged to follow suit, Andrews led Saundby after Hawker and was then attacked from above. Andrews fired a short burst at a machine on Hawker's tail, forcing it to break away. He then had his fuel tank and engine hit and was saved from being shot down by the intervention of Saundby, who chased the enemy machine off Andrew's tail. Hawker was last seen circling in combat below.

Von Richthofen described the battle in his autobiography, *The Red Air Fighter*, thus:

> *I was extremely proud when one fine day I was informed that the aviator whom I had brought down on 23rd November1916 was the English Immelmann.*

> *In view of the character of our fight it was clear to me that I had been tackling a flying champion.*

> *One day I was blithely flying to give chase when I noticed three Englishmen who also had apparently gone a-hunting. I noticed that they were interested in my direction, and as I felt much inclination to have a fight I did not want to disappoint them.*

> *I was flying at a lower altitude. Consequently I had to wait until one of my English friends tried to drop on me. After a short while he came sailing along and wanted to tackle me in the rear. After firing five shots he had to stop, for I had swerved in a sharp curve.*

> *The Englishman tried to catch me up in the rear while I tried to get behind him. So we circled round and round like madmen after one another at an altitude of about10,000 feet.*

> *First we circled twenty times to the left, and then thirty times to the right. Each tried to get behind and above the other.*

> *Soon I discovered I was not meeting a beginner. He had not the slightest intention to break off the fight. He was travelling in a box which turned beautifully. However, my packing case was better at climbing than his. But I succeeded at last in getting above and beyond my English waltzing partner.*

> *When we had got down to about 6,000 feet without having achieved anything particular, my opponent ought to have*

At about 2.0 p.m.
"I attacked 9 H.A.
just N.E. (BAPAUME) +
drove them E. when
I observed 2 strong
patrols of HA. scouts
above me.. I was
about to abandon
the pursuit when
a de H. Scout Maj.
Hawker dived passed
me & continued to pursue.
We were at once attacked
by the HA., one of which
dived on to Maj. Hawker's
tail. I drove him off
firing about 25 rounds
at close range. My
engine was immediately

shot thro' from
behind + I was
obliged to dry +
regain our lines.
When on the lines another
de Haw. came diving
past me from the side
+ drove the HA. off
my tail. I
last saw Maj. Hawker
at about 3,000 near
BAPAUME, spiralling
down fighting with an
HA. apparently under
control but going down.

---

discovered that it was time for him to take his leave. The wind was favourable to me, for it drove us more and more towards the German positions. At last we were above Bapaume, about half a mile behind the German front. The gallant fellow was full of pluck, and when we had got down to about 3,000 feet he merrily waved to me as if he would say, Well, how do you do?

The circles which we made around one another were so narrow that their diameter was probably no more than 250 or 300 feet. I had time to take a good look at my opponent. I looked down into his carriage and could see every movement of his head. If he had not had his cap on I would have noticed what kind of face he was making.

My Englishman was a good sportsman, but by and by the thing became a little too hot for him. He had to decide whether he would land on German ground or whether he would fly back to the English lines. Of course he tried the latter, after having endeavoured in vain to escape me by loopings and such tricks. At the time his first bullets were flying around me, for so far neither of us had been able to do any shooting.

When he had come down to about 300 feet he tried to escape by flying a zig-zag course, which makes it difficult for an observer on the ground to shoot. That was my most favourable moment. I followed him at an altitude of from 250 feet to 150 feet, firing all the time. The Englishman could not avoid falling. But the jamming of my gun nearly robbed me of my success.

My opponent fell shot through the head 150 feet behind our line. His machine gun was dug

J O Andrew's report of the action in which Hawker was lost.

84

Picture No. 15. A view looking across the east aerodrome. The remains of 21 Squadron's BE12s after a gale on 29 August 1916.

out of the ground and it ornaments the entrance of my dwelling. Hawker fell near the shell-shattered ruins of Luisenhof Farm, two miles south of Bapaume. He was buried where he fell by German infantry, but with the ground constantly churned up by shelling, his grave was subsequently lost. His name is one of a thousand commemorated on the Air Services Memorial to the Missing at Arras.

Epitaph for Hawker

On 26 May 1968, a window was dedicated to Lanoe Hawker at Longparish Church in Hampshire. The address was read by R H M S Saundby, a member of that fatal last patrol but now, after a distinguished career, Air Marshal Sir Robert Saundby KCB, KBE, MC, DFC, AFC:

> *Most of us once or twice in a life-time, fall under the spell of some-one whose outstanding personality and character stimulate and inspire us. Such people can lift us up, and very often they have a deep and lasting influence on our lives.*
>
> *In whatever walk of life they may be found, such people are recognised as natural leaders.*
>
> *I was fortunate in that I met such a man while I was yet young. Perhaps most of us do, before cynicism and scepticism have tended to cloud our judgement and harden our hearts.*
>
> *At the age of 20 I was posted to No.24 (Fighter) Squadron, at a time the ghastly Battle of the Somme was just beginning. The squadron was stationed on an aerodrome at Bertangles, a little vignette of which appears at the foot of the memorial window.*

24 Squadron Officer's Mess at Bertangles in the ubiquitous Nissen hut.

Tented accommodation for 24 Squadron hidden in the woods at Bertangles

There I met the squadron's Commanding Officer, Major Lanoe Hawker. He was the first man in the Royal Flying Corps to gain the V.C. and the D.S.O. and I regarded him with awe and admiration. But as time passed the admiration increased while the awe gave way to respect and affection.

Hawker had all the qualities that I then most admired, and which I admire still. He was, it goes without saying, superbly courageous, but that in itself can mean but little. More to the point, he was conscientious, reasonable, fair and just, and remarkably modest.

When a pilot became due for leave his thoughts turned to home and family, to friends and all the old familiar places, which on the Western Front seemed at times so very far off and unattainable. The last patrol before going on leave was always an anxious time. How frightful if, at the last moment, something happened that would dash the cup from one's lips.

It was an order that Squadron Commanders should fly over the lines only in exceptional circumstances, But Hawker,

86

whenever his duties permitted, would turn up just before a patrol was due to take off, and say to such a one, "Cut along now, and start your leave. I am taking your place". The young pilot, overwhelmed with relief and gratitude, would set off for home with a light heart.

But it was this considerate habit that led to Hawker's death. On November 23rd, he dismissed a young pilot about to go on leave, and took his place. There were three of us on the patrol, of which I was one. We were set upon by Richthofen's Circus, and in the ensuing "dogfight" against heavy odds, we became separated. Hawker, after a tremendous fight with the redoubtable baron, was shot down and killed on the enemy side of the lines. J.O. Andrews, the Flight Commander and patrol leader, was also shot down, but he was unhurt and managed to get down on our side of the lines.

How well I remember that wintry evening, nearly 52 years ago. Hawker had not returned, but so great was our faith in his ability and fighting experience, that none of us doubted that he would turn up somehow. As dusk fell we lit the landing flares, and kept them burning all night. But when dawn came with no word from him, our hopes began to fade.

It was days before we could believe that he had gone from us, but we hoped he was a prisoner of war.

One week earlier, on November 17th, my younger brother had been reported missing, believed killed, in 29 (Fighter) Squadron. The loss of Hawker, coming so soon afterwards, made me so unhappy that I did not care whether I lived or died.

But the young are resilient, and in time I overcame these feelings, I began to understand how great the influence of Hawker had been and, even more important, to realize that though the man himself had gone, the influence lived on. His courage and determination, his unselfishness and understanding, and his gaiety and modesty had its effect on all who knew him, and on very many who did not.

He died young, at the height of his glory, but his example became enshrined in the traditions of the Royal Air Force, and helped to give our fighter pilots, 24 years later, the courage and endurance to prevail against great odds in the Battle of Britain.

It is fitting that this beautiful memorial window should be in this church, which the Hawker family had known so well for so many generations.

Whenever I think of Lanoe Hawker I am reminded of the tribute paid to Brutus in the closing scenes of Julius Caesar:
"His life was gentle, and the elements
So mixed in him that Nature might stand up,
And say to all the world, This was a man"

Latter days of 24 Squadron

Number 24 was to serve again at Bertangles, albeit on the other side of the field they occupied in 1916. During the retreat of March 1918 they were only here for two days but returned in August and remained for a month. Their 'star turn' in 1918, and a worthy successor to the likes of J O Andrews and Lanoe Hawker, was Captain Tom Falcon Hazell.

Born in 1892 Hazell was from County Galway in Ireland and had been educated at Tonbridge School. On the outbreak of war he joined the Royal Inniskilling Fusiliers and served with them until June 1916, when he transferred to the RFC. He joined 1 Squadron at Bailleul, claiming twenty German machines and being awarded a Military Cross.

After a spell at home instructing, he then joined 24 Squadron in June 1918 as the commander of A Flight. In the next three months he claimed another 23 enemy aircraft, including ten balloons and

Captain T F Hazell, DSO, MC, DFC and Bar, A Flight Commander 24 Squadron.

Hazell's SE5a, B8422, being dismantled after his encounter with Udet on 22 August 1918.

was awarded the DSO, DFC and Bar. In *A History of 24 Squadron Royal Air Force* by Captain A E Illingworth, there are recorded two actions in August 1918 during which Hazell brought down balloons a week after arriving at Bertangles:

August 21st. - This is a very hot and dusty camp. Hazell put up a very fine show to-day after balloons, circling round the top of one while rectifying machine gun trouble, in such a way that he could not be shot at from the ground, and then shooting down another.

August 22nd. - We are pushing north of the Somme today. Hazell again put up a marvellous show when sent out to keep balloons down, and deliberately shot one down under the very noses of its escort of seven Fokkers, which afterwards came down and riddled his machine with holes - petrol tank first shot - then his propeller and two longerons, in spite of which he fought his way back with eyes full of petrol, and landed in the aerodrome within thirty minutes of starting off.

The squadron record book commented, *Capt Hazell was seen home by the EA who shot his tank, longerons and propeller to pieces.*

This was probably one of the few occasions in the war where top aces encountered each other as it seems that Hazell had run into *Jasta* 4 led by *Leutnant* Ernst Udet, who was the highest scoring German ace to survive the war. Hazell at this time had claimed nearly forty German aircraft but was himself credited to Udet as his sixtieth victory. In the English translation of his autobiography *Mein Fliegerleben*, published as *Ace of the Iron Cross*, he wrote of this encounter:

An excited voice on the telephone: "Two balloons have just been shot down here. The enemy squadron is still circling over our position."

We take off at once, the entire fourth Staffel with all available machines. We head towards Braie at three thousand metres altitude. Below us the chain of German balloons, obliquely above us the British squadron, five SE5's. We stay below them and wait for their attack. But they hang on and seem to be avoiding a fight.

Suddenly, one of them darts past me down towards the balloons. I push down and go after him. It is their leader. The narrow streamer flaps in front of me. I push down, down, down. The air screams at the windshield. I must catch him, stop him from getting to the balloons.

Too late! The shadow of his aircraft flits across the taut skin

Leutnant Ernst Udet, commanding officer of *Jasta* 4 in front of his Fokker DVII.

of the balloon like a fish through shallow water. A small blue flame licks out and creeps slowly across its back. At the next moment a fountain of fire shoots up where, just a moment ago, the golden yellow bag had floated with a silken glow.

A German Fokker comes at the Englishman; a second, smaller fireball lights up alongside the larger one, and the German aircraft hits the ground wrapped in smoke and flame.

In a very tight turn, the Englishman goes almost straight down. The troops at the balloon cable winch scatter, but the S.E.5 has already flattened out and sweeps westward, hugging the ground. He is down so low that the machine and its shadow merge into one. But now I am on his tail and a wild chase begins, hardly three metres above ground. We hop telegraph poles and dodge trees. A mighty jump, the church steeple of Marécourt, but I hang on to him. I'm not about to let go.

The main highway to Arras. Flanked by high trees, it winds through the landscape like a green wall. He flies to the right of the trees, I to the left. Every time there is a gap in the trees I fire. Alongside the road, on a meadow, German infantry is camped. Although I am on his neck, he fires at them. This is his undoing.

At that moment I jump the treetops - hardly ten metres separate us - and fire. A tremor runs through his machine; it wavers, tumbles into a spin, hits the ground, bounces up again like a stone rebounding from the water, and disappears in a mighty hop behind a small birch grove. A dust cloud rises.

Perspiration is running across my face, and it fogs my goggles. I wipe my forehead with my sleeve. It is midsummer, August 22, 12:30 p.m., the hottest day of the year. Almost forty

90

degrees centigrade, and during the pursuit my motor ran at 1600rpm.

I look around and see three S.E.5's. They have shaken off my squadron and are diving on me to avenge their dead leader. Close to the ground, I chase around the birch grove. I take short, quick looks over my shoulder. They are splitting up, two turning off to the west, leaving me to one of them.

I know now that I am dealing with tactically tried and proven opponents. Beginners would have come at me in a bunch. Old fighter pilots know that during a pursuit you only get in each other's way.

Things are looking bad for me. The other works himself in toward me. I estimate the distance barely thirty metres but still he does not fire. "He wants to finish me off with three or four rounds," I figure.

The landscape consists of gently rolling hills dotted with small groves. I curve round these groves. Among the trees I spot a German machine gun unit. They stare up at us. "If they would only shoot to release me from my predicament." But they don't fire. Perhaps we are too close together, perhaps they are afraid they might hit me in the constant up and down. I take in the landscape. So this is where I will fall!

Then I feel a light, dull blow at my knee. I look down and notice the sweet, faint odour of phosphorous and a hole in the ammunition case. The heat - the phosphorous ammunition has ignited itself -in a matter of seconds, my aircraft will be in flames.

In a situation like this, one doesn't think. One acts or dies. A squeeze on the machine gun trigger and from both barrels the ammunition stabs out into the blue sky, trailing white smoke.

A look over my shoulder, breathless surprise, and then a few deep, lung-filling breaths. The enemy turns away, avoiding the white smoke trails. He probably thinks I am firing backwards. I fly home.

After touching down I remain seated in the cockpit for quite a while. Behrend has to help me out of the machine. I go to the orderly room.

"Oberleutnant Goering is coming tonight," says the sergeant. I look at him with empty eyes.

"Goering, our new C.O.," he repeats.

"Yes, Yes." My own voice sounds strange to me. I want to go

on furlough. At once. Right away. He must not see me this way.
Despite what Udet thought he had seen, in fact Hazell returned to Bertangles, though his machine had to be dismantled and returned to the depot for repair. Some days later, it was struck off charge of the RAF as not worth repairing.

Hazell ended the war as commanding officer of 203 Squadron and remained in the RAF until retiring in 1927 as a Squadron Leader. He died in 1946.

Continue along the D97 into Bertangles village. Where the road turns sharply right turn left and the cemetery is a short distance along this road on the left.

Bertangles Communal Cemetery

For details of the action in which von Richthofen was killed go to the Morlancourt Ridge entry at the end of Chapter Two.

Major Sholto Douglas, in command of 84 Squadron at Bertangles, recorded his memories of the death of von Richthofen and his subsequent burial. He begins with the return of Roy Brown and the other members of 209 Squadron:

When he (Brown) had returned to Bertangles that Sunday morning he put in a report about the combat, but he did not know

Picture No. 16. The wreckage of von Richthofen's triplane behind No. 3 Squadron Australian Flying Corps' hangars at Bertangles. By the time the souvenir hunters had finished there was little left. On the extreme right of the photograph is Captain A F W Beauchamp Proctor VC, DSO, MC and Bar, DFC of 84 Squadron.

Picture No. 17. The funeral cortege leaves 3 AFC's hangars on the late afternoon of 22 April 1918.

until afterwards that it was Richthofen whom he had shot down. By then the excitement was intense, and when the remains of the Fokker triplane and Richthofen's body were brought in there was immense curiosity.

The only suitable place to keep the body of Richthofen was a canvas hangar belonging to my squadron that happened to be empty. He was laid out in the hangar on a small raised platform, and many of us went to see him as he rested there more or less in state. It was a curious experience, after all we had heard about him, to see him lying there. The next day he was buried with full military honours in the local cemetery at Bertangles, alongside the airfield. The escort and the final salute were provided by the Australians, who were claiming that their people had shot down Richthofen from the ground.

It was with mixed feelings that I watched the burial of the great German ace, for it was impossible not to feel a little emotional about it. Richthofen was the most successful, in actual scoring, of all the fighter pilots of the First World War. I thought about what he had achieved, and I wondered, as I have many times since, just what sort of man he was. Richthofen was undoubtedly a gallant pilot, although he always fought with the utmost caution - except for his very last scrap - and he never hesitated to avoid a fight or pull out of one if he thought that the odds against him were too great.

Von Richthofen was given, by the standards of the First World War, an elaborate funeral. In fact it was compared unfavourably with the

Picture No. 19. Bertangles cemetery in 1999.

funeral of James McCudden, Britain's foremost ace at his death, which was a simple, hurried, if not bodged, affair. Von Richthofen's coffin left 3 Squadron Australian Flying Corps' hangars at Bertangles aerodrome on the back of a Crossley tender, escorted by personnel of the same squadron. The pallbearers were also officers from 3 AFC. At the graveside there was a firing party and a large crowd of onlookers.

The burial of von Richthofen was not popular with the inhabitants of the village of Bertangles and his body was later moved to the German cemetery at Fricourt. In 1925 his body was moved yet again to Berlin, where there was an elaborate state funeral, though his family wanted him returned to Schweidnitz, the family home. In the 1970s the cemetery (or *Invalidenfriedhof*) was very close, in fact too close, to the Berlin Wall and the East Germans wanted to clear the area. Several aces and heroes' graves were lost in the clearing of part of the cemetery, including that of Ernst Udet, Germany's second most

Picture No. 18. The funeral of Manfred von Richthofen on 22 April 1918.

successful fighter pilot of the First World War, though it has recently been found again.

Von Richthofen's family were able to have Manfred's coffin delivered to the West, where he now lies next to his mother, sister and younger brother in the family plot at Wiesbaden.

Postscript

Today there is only one Commonwealth War Graves Commission headstone in Bertangles cemetery. James Arthur Miller crashed on take off as 24 Squadron left Bertangles for their new aerodrome at Conteville on 28 March 1918. He had come all the way from the USA and had only been in the squadron for twenty- six days.

Return to the centre of the village and follow the signs to Amiens. On reaching the N25 turn right towards Amiens. At the roundabout at Poulainville turn left into the village. Just past the church turn left for about 300 metres and then turn right on the C17 to Allonville. Cross the D11 and continue towards Allonville. Turn right down the D247 and then after a short distance turn left onto the D919. Proceed along this road until Hedauville and turn left on the D938 to Forceville. The cemetery is located just north of the village on the left side of the road.

Forceville Communal Cemetery Extension

The graves we have come to see are in the far left corner of the cemetery near the Stone of Remembrance.

Forceville Communal Cemetery Extension (9/58), designed by Sir Reginald Blomfield, was one of the three prototype cemeteries built by War Graves before they standardised on the design we are familiar with today.

In the Ypres area there are a number of German aviators whose graves are maintained in Commonwealth War Graves Commission cemeteries. On the Somme battlefield there are very few and there have been suggestions that there might have been a deliberate policy to remove all other nationalities from Commonwealth War Graves cemeteries in the vicinity. Possibly only two German air service casualties lie in CWGC burial grounds on the Somme. The two graves in this cemetery are of particular interest, as they are not only from early in the air war but are linked to Captain L W B Rees, whom we met earlier in the chapter at Vert Galand.

A third grave we have come to visit was a result of the first ever, official victory claimed by a *Jagdstaffel*.

Fritz Kölpin and Ernst Leonhardi of *FA* 23 (III A2 and A1)

Lionel Wilmot Brabazon Rees had joined 11 Squadron in February 1915 and as related earlier had gone out to France ahead of the squadron to prepare for their arrival. He was also in charge of the party that repaired Gilbert Insall's Vickers FB5 at the conclusion of the incident for which the latter earned his Victoria Cross. (See the Bertangles entry for this action.) During the summer of 1915 Rees aggressively waged war on the German Air Service, attacking enemy machines at every opportunity. On 31 August 1915, together with Flight Sergeant J M Hargreaves, he had fought with a German two-seater for 45 minutes before running out

Captain L W B Rees, 11 Squadron, shown here wearing his VC and MC ribbons as a Major.

of ammunition. Returning for more ammunition he took off and shot down the enemy aeroplane. Further combats occurred in September, including one on 21 September.

This engagement was described by Hargreaves in an article in the August 1933 edition of the magazine *Popular Flying*. It gives an idea of the skill necessary for what most people would consider mundane photo-reconnaissance work. Hargreaves was working in a shallow, cramped, nacelle, buffeted by the icy blast of the slipstream, encumbered by bulky flying clothing and handling heavy glass negatives with thick clumsy gloves. If that was not enough, he was then obliged to operate his unwieldy Lewis machine gun during an attack on a German aeroplane.

Our machine was the old Vickers fighter which lent itself admirably for photographic and fighting duties. On this particular occasion we had to photograph the German front line trenches from Peronne to Esterre, South of the Somme or as much of it as we could cover with 18 plates.

After the usual examination to see that everything was in order - gun, ammunition, maps, camera, plates, etc., etc - we were started up and set off for the northern section of the line - Peronne, from which end we had decided to work. I arranged with the pilot that we should patrol the line twice to enable me to work out the central objective of each succeeding photograph. Naturally for the first picture I was all ready and set, hanging over the front just waiting to reach the perpendicular line over the pre-arranged objective. This successfully accomplished, I quickly reloaded and just managed to get over in time to take the second objective. By the time I had performed the changing of plates, etc., and got over the front again I found that we had overshot our third objective. Without hesitation, I knelt up and swung my head round in circular manner to indicate to my pilot that we had gone too far. To my great satisfaction he immediately heeled over and retraced our path, so that I had ample time to pick up my third objective. This operation had to be repeated several times, but without any prearrangement my pilot had grasped the situation perfectly.

Our third trip along the line brought us hundreds of greetings from our dear old friends, the "Archies". Their efforts were persistent and fairly accurate.

Much credit was due to Capt. Rees, who performed all sorts of misleading evolutions to the watchful eyes of "Archies" attendants.

Without hitch or hindrance we shot every plate successfully. Before commencing operations each plate was carefully numbered and arranged, so that numbers 1, 2, 3, etc., should correspond exactly to that particular section on the country below, but in spite of the careful survey of equipment before leaving the aerodrome I found that after the first exposure I had forgotten to hang up an empty plate bag to receive them when finished.

Having no receptacle to receive them I was compelled to place them on the floor of the machine in front of me. This caused me considerable inconvenience when getting over the front again; I had to keep pushing them forward away from my knees. Just after completion and before I had time to collect the scattered plates from the floor of the nacelle, Capt. Rees drew my attention to a machine coming up from the German lines with the obvious intention of pushing us off or at least shaking our morale. My pilot immediately switched his engine off and glided down towards the German. After dropping about 2,000 feet we were slightly above it and about 200 yards apart; we could clearly see that she was a new bus and vastly different from anything we had encountered before. They fired several bursts from about 200 yards to 100 yards range but fortunately for us, without effect. When the range had slightly decreased I opened up with half a drum, which must have resulted in some vital damage, for the machine immediately turned into a glide outwards and headed for their own lines, where she apparently crashed on landing.

A little more than a week later, on 30 September Rees and Hargreaves ran into an Albatros two-seater of *FA* 23 flown by *Leutnant* Fritz Kölpin and *Oberleutnant* Ernst Leonhardi. Storming into the attack the German machine was riddled. Kölpin, the pilot, was hit in the head and then the right wings ripped off. The wreckage fell to the ground near Gommecourt. At the end of October Rees was awarded a well deserved MC and Hargreaves the DCM. (For more information about Hargreaves see the Villers-Bretonneux Aerodrome 1915 entry in the next chapter.)

In November Rees was posted home and promoted to command No. 32 Squadron, forming up for service in France. He was to earn the Victoria Cross during his next period in France and we shall meet him again at Treizennes, an aerodrome south of Hazebrouck. (See *Airfields and Airmen: The Channel Coast.*)

Airman First Class H P Warminger (III B3)

The first *Jagdstaffel* formed was, in fact *Jasta* 2, on 10 August 1916, and the second, which came into existence on 22 August 1916, was *Jasta* 1. This unit was made up of personnel from *Flieger Ersatz Abteilung 7 (FEA 7), KEK* Nord and other units in the area. On 22 August 1916 *Offizierstellvertreter* Leopold Reimann brought down a Sopwith 11/2 Strutter of 70 Squadron flown by Second Lieutenant A M Vaucour and Lieutenant A J Bott. The machine forced landed in the British lines and neither man was injured.

The following day Vaucour returned to the machine with Air Mechanic Warminger to effect repairs. Herbert Percy Warminger, born in Jarrow, Durham, had joined the RFC on 10 February 1915, in Sunderland and prior to this was a farmer. He had served in the Durham Fortress Royal Engineers for four years and, at the age of 26, was older than most.

After rectification the machine was flown back with Warminger as a passenger in the rear seat. Unfortunately, they were attacked by three enemy machines southwest of Albert and then hit in the fuel tank by anti-aircraft fire. At the same time Warminger was hit by a shell splinter. Vaucour managed to get back to 70 Squadron's aerodrome at Fienvillers, eight kilometres southwest of Doullens but Warminger later died of his wounds.

MESSAGES AND SIGNALS.

Army Form C. 2123.

No of Message ___

Charges to Pay. £ s. d.

Office Stamp.

277

571

Service Instructions. ___

Handed in at ___

TO H.Q., R.F.C.   Office ___ m. Received 6.25 p.

Sender's Number G 118   Day of Month 30   In reply to Number ___

AAA

Reference	report	of	Captain	combat	AAA
the air	by			REES	in
report	that	Captain		guns	and
down	German	A.A.	machine		brought
AAA	Further	investigation	this		morning
doubt	that	the	leaves		no
brought	down	by	Albatross		was
AAA	Pilot	of	Captain		REES
shot	through		Albatross		was
gun	bullets	head	with		Lewis
also	hit	and	observer		was
and	remains	AAA	Benz		Engine
in	3rd	of	machine		are
Machine	pillaged	Aircraft	Park		AAA
troops	before	and	wrecked		by
		R.F.C.	officers		arrived

FROM
PLACE & TIME O.C. 3rd Wing.

6.25 p.m.

Received 6.30 p.m.

This message shows that anti-aircraft fire also claimed Kölpin and Leonhardi.

For further details of the first *Jasta* victory and Leopold Reimann, see the Frasnoy German Cemetery entry in Chapter One of *Airfields and Airmen: Cambrai*.

Return to Forceville village and continue on the D938 into Albert. This concludes the first aviation tour of the Somme area.

The Southern Area

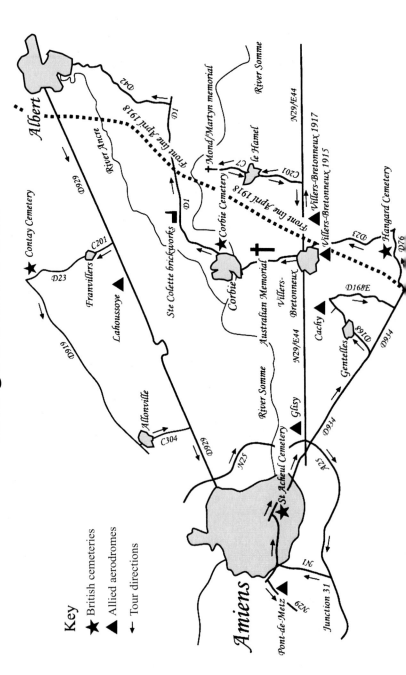

Key
★ British cemeteries
▲ Allied aerodromes
← Tour directions

Albert

D42
D1
River Ancre
Front line April 1918
D929
Contay Cemetery
C201
Franvillers
Lahoussoye
D23
D919
Ste Colette brickworks
D1
Allonville
C304
D929
N25

Mond/Martyn memorial
River Somme
le Hamel
C7
C201
Corbie Cemetery
Front line April 1918
Corbie
Australian Memorial
Villers-Bretonneux
N29/E44
River Somme
Glisy
D934
Gentelles
D168
D168E
Cachy
N25
St Acheul Cemetery

N29/E44
Villers-Bretonneux 1917
Villers-Bretonneux 1915
Villers-Bretonneux
Hangard Cemetery
D23
D76
D934

Amiens
Pont-de-Metz
N29
Junction 31
N1

Chapter Two

SOMME: THE SOUTHERN AREA

This area also remained mainly in Allied hands until the great German offensive in the spring of 1918. The limit of the German advance was Villers-Bretonneux, where they were held by a fierce Allied defence. The spot is now marked by the impressive Australian National Memorial. The places that will be visited, together with the principal points of interest, are:

Contay British Military Cemetery - Major J C Callaghan of 87 Squadron
Amiens aerodrome - the first RFC machine to land in France
St Acheul French National Cemetery - the first RFC casualties
Cachy aerodrome - *Groupe de Combat* 12, *Lafayette Escadrill*e
Hangard Communal Cemetery Extension - S C Welinkar of 23 Squadron
Le Hamel - a memorial to F L Mond and E M Martyn of 57 Squadron
Villers-Bretonneux Aerodrome - the 1915 RFC aerodrome
Villers-Bretonneux Aerodrome - the 1917 aerodrome
Villers-Bretonneux Military Cemetery - bombing casualties
Morlancourt Ridge - von Richthofen's crash site

Leave Albert on the D929 to Amiens and turn right after approximately six kilometres turn right on the C201 to Franvillers. In Franvillers turn right on the D23 to Contay. The cemetery is on the right side of the road before you enter the village.

Contay British Military Cemetery

In August 1916 this spot was chosen for 49 Casualty Clearing Station and the following month it was joined by 9 Casualty Clearing Station. With the German withdrawal to the Hindenburg Line in March 1917, the Clearing Stations moved further east. The cemetery (9/94) came back into use in April, with the Allied retreat, and the last burial here was in August 1918.

Major J C Callaghan's grave is in the far left corner against the hornbeam hedge. There are lovely mature lime trees either side of the Cross of Sacrifice.

Major Joseph Creuss Callaghan (IX A14)

Major J C Callaghan MC, commanding 87 Squadron.

The death of J C Callaghan on 2 July 1918, brought the final tragedy to a family who had suffered appallingly during the Great War. He was the eldest of three brothers all of whom were killed while in the RFC or RAF. It is difficult to imagine what the loss of all your sons must be like. The second son, Stanislaus Creuss Callaghan or Stan as he was known, was killed in an accident in Canada during training on 27 June 1917, and is buried at Barrie, Ontario. The youngest son, Eugene Creuss Callaghan, known as Owen, had gone missing on 26 August 1916, with 19 Squadron. It was a black day for 19 Squadron as five machines failed to return from a bombing mission. It was believed they became lost in a storm and of the five pilots lost, three died. Callaghan has no known grave and is commemorated on the Air Services Memorial at Arras.

Joseph Creuss Callaghan, known to his friends as Casey, was born in 1892. After studying at Belvedere College, Dublin he then went to Stonyhurst. After service in the Royal Munster Fusiliers he joined the RFC. Initial flying training was conducted at Norwich and then he was sent to the Central Flying School. His first operational posting was to 18 Squadron RFC on 1 February 1916, initially flying the Vickers FB5 two-seater scout.

On 26 April he and his gunner, Second Lieutenant James Mitchell, were returning from a photographic patrol in an FE2b, when they saw four enemy machines approaching from the direction of Arras. In the ensuing fight Mitchell fired half a drum of ammunition into a Fokker monoplane. Another Fokker attacked from the rear and disabled the engine, in addition to destroying the elevator control. Mitchell was hit in the head and killed. The FE2, though without any pitch control, maintained a stable glide angle and eventually a reasonable landing was made. Mitchell, from Montreal and an old man at age 34 is buried in Bruay Communal Cemetery Extension.

In June Callaghan was promoted to flight commander. Though wounded on 31 July, he remained with the unit until posted home in November 1916, having been awarded an MC. His Military Cross was awarded for general good work, including a number of night-bombing operations, where on one occasion he shot out a searchlight.

For all of 1917 he remained in training units and was then posted

Sopwith Dolphin D3775 'N' of 87 Squadron, with Lieutenant Golding. The horizontal 'S' was the squadron marking allotted on 22 March 1918.

to command No. 87 Squadron at Hounslow in February 1918. They were equipping with the new Sopwith Dolphin ready for service in France. The Dolphin has been a much under-rated aeroplane and only four RFC/RAF squadrons on the Western Front were to receive it. The last of the four was 87 Squadron, who crossed to France on 24 April 1918 under Callaghan's leadership.

Together with many other commanding officers, he was not content to sit on the ground and joined in patrols, during which he successfully brought down four enemy aircraft.

On 2 July 1918, Major Callaghan left at 1015 hours for a Special Patrol and was shot down in flames over Albert. He was seen to attack a formation of Fokker DVIIs single handed. The squadron had done very well, as they had been at the Front for over two months without suffering a combat casualty. Unfortunately, their commanding officer was the first loss. Another member of the squadron described the fight:

He was last seen with a patrol of 60 Squadron, and then a tremendous fight started, and he went into the thick of it, as he always would. Captain Maxwell in 56 Squadron, saw one machine fighting about twenty-five Germans, but the machine was hit before he could arrive close enough. I am afraid there is no doubt as to who was the pilot of that machine. He was so absurdly gallant and so absolutely without any idea of fear, that he would cheerfully take on any kind of odds. We had all implored him not to go about by himself and run such risks, but I don't think he realised that he could ever find a Hun or any number of Huns that he wasn't a match for.

We have lost in him one of the finest squadron commanders, and one of the finest fighting pilots on the Western Front to-day, and as such he cannot be replaced. But to us his loss is even more irreplaceable. We feel that we have lost a great stout-hearted friend, always ready to help anybody out of trouble, a gallant companion in a fight, and a sportsman to the backbone.

Continue into Contay and in the village centre turn left on the D919, signposted to Amiens. In Allonville turn left on the C304 to Camon. At the traffic lights on the D929 turn right towards Amiens. At the roundabout turn onto the N25 signposted to Longeau and Paris. This is the Amiens ring road and the N25 eventually becomes the A29. Leave the A29 at junction 31, the N1 to Amiens. After approximately one and a half kilometres turn left at the traffic lights onto the NI signposted to Rouen (the Boulevard de Chateaudun). At the roundabout turn left onto the N29 to Rouen. You will eventually reach a set of traffic lights with a sign to the Hospital Sud. Turn left here (D408). After a short distance you will reach a roundabout. Continue round and stop where marked on the aerodrome plan. This is the historic 1914 Amiens aerodrome.

Amiens Aerodrome
Pont-de-Metz

Amiens is the capital of the Somme *département* and the largest city in the area. During the First World War it was a major communications and supply centre for the British army and therefore, an important objective for the German army.

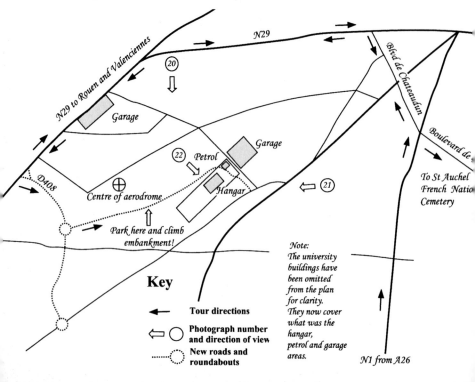

Picture No. 20. Pont-de-Metz aerodrome looking to the south.

Picture No. 21. Pont-de-Metz looking to the west.

It has been assumed that the present Amiens aerodome at Glisy was the one upon which the RFC made their historic first landing on active service. However, Glisy was not completed until just before the start of the Second World War, just in time to be used by the Luftwaffe and is probably the third, if not fourth, flying field the city has had.

The first Amiens aerodrome at Pont-de-Metz is historic for two reasons. Not only was it the site of the first landing by the RFC on active service but also where the first casualties of the RFC and the British army occurred in France.

Pont-de-Metz Aerodrome

It is unlikely that students driving from the Rue de Rouen to their university campus at Pont-de-Metz, in the southern suburbs of Amiens, realise what an historic site the open field is on their left. For in the late summer of 1914 the Royal Flying Corps landed here, going to war for the first time. The first faltering steps of what by the end of 1918 had become the largest air force in the world, with 27,000 officers, 290,000 men and over 20,000 aeroplanes. They set the trend and traditions for the Royal Air Force, which became a massive instrument of power during the Second World War.

Aviation first came to Amiens in May 1909, when an aeroplane flew from the hippodrome at Petite-Saint-Jean, about two kilometres southwest of the city centre. On 15, 16 and 17 August 1910 further flying was carried out at a military site at Montjoie, approximately four kilometres due south of the city. This location was designated as an emergency landing ground by the RFC during the desperate fighting of spring 1918. On 7 July 1911, land was taken over adjacent to the Rue de Rouen, not far from the hippodrome. A public subscription was initiated by René Ransson, the *Président de la Société Aérienne de Picardie* for military aviation in the region. A hangar was erected at Pont-de-Metz and accepted on 15 July 1912, by *M le Général* Picquart, commanding the 2 *Corps d'Armée*. The aerodrome was transferred to the Ministry of War a year later, on 28 August 1912.

Picture No. 22. The 1912 military hangar at Amiens (Pont-de-Metz) aerodrome.

The RFC arrive

From the Development of Military Flying section at the beginning of the book the visitor will have read how well prepared the RFC were at the outbreak of war.

In his delightful autobiography, *Flying Corps HQ 1914 - 1918*, Maurice Baring wrote of this time. He had only joined the RFC on 9 August and received his uniform on the day he embarked for France. Baring was well-travelled and knew seven languages. He was appointed a lieutenant in the Intelligence Corps attached to the RFC, though he had no idea of his duties. On joining the flying services he had no idea of the existence of the RFC! He eventually became the personal assistant to General Hugh Trenchard for most of the war. Baring wrote:

We arrived at Amiens at 12 o'clock and reported to the French authorities. Longcroft wanted to go up to the Aerodrome at once. This upset the French authorities who said they had not yet had their déjeuner. Here for the first time we came onto contact with one sacred, almost appalling fact, whatever happens, the French nation must not be disturbed during the hour of their mid-day meal. Whatever happens they must have their déjeuner at the appointed hour and the rite must not be disturbed nor curtailed. We learned this lesson on August 12th. Longcroft and Salmond, in spite of their impatience to get to work at once, were obliged to wait until the hour of déjeuner was over.

After luncheon we went up to the Aerodrome and found what was necessary for us to get. We had to arrange many things. Water carts had to be obtained, pegs for the aeroplanes and many other things, also a certain consignment of B.B. Oil had to be found in the station. We spent that afternoon interviewing various people, who promised to get what we wanted, and various officials at the railway stations (there were two stations) on the subject of B.B.Oil.

We slept in our valises on the grass of the Aerodrome. We awoke with the dawn and bathed in the dew. A small crowd watched the operations and cheered.

Sefton Brancker, one of the officers in the Royal Flying Corps who remained in England, also related this incident:

Incidentally Maurice Baring startled the inhabitants on the morning following their arrival by rolling in the dew on Amiens aerodrome as a substitute for a bath! This was the first introduction of Amiens to the "mad English".

Sefton Brancker, later Air Vice-Marshal Sir Sefton Brancker, Director of Civil Aviation. Killed in the R101 airship disaster on 5 October 1930.

The machines of 2, 3 and 4 Squadrons concentrated at Dover on the evening of 12 August and at midnight Lieutenant Colonel F H Sykes, commanding the RFC, arrived and gave orders for all machines to be ready to depart at six o'clock in the morning. The first machine took off at 0625 hours for this historic flight, the first deployment of the RFC overseas.

One of the officers who made this flight was P B Joubert de la Ferté, a flight commander in No. 3 Squadron (later Air Chief Marshal Sir Philip Joubert KCB, CMG, DSO.) In his autobiography *The Fated Sky* he wrote:

Next morning we were served out with a motor-car tyre inner tube which we were instructed to blow up and wear round our middles in case we fell into the "Drink" on our way to France. It was as well that nobody had to try out this primitive life-saving device, which was certainly very difficult to wear in the tiny cockpits of the aircraft of the day. As he crossed the French coast one pilot found the Cape Gris-Nez lighthouse so inviting an object that he spent a little time trying to drop his inner tube, like a quoit, on to the spiky top. There was a good deal of competition as to who should land first in France.

Harvey-Kelly, the first RFC pilot to land in France

The operation was led by the senior squadron commander, Major C J Burke, commanding No. 2 Squadron, who was undoubtedly aware of the significance of this flight, and who intended to be the first to land on foreign soil. No. 2 Squadron had already had an epic start to their preparations, as they had flown down from their peace-time station at

H D Harvey-Kelly having a cigarette by his BE2, No. 347, somewhere en-route to or from Montrose, where 2 Squadron were based.

Montrose in Scotland. However, things were not to go according to plan, as Sefton Brancker related:

Burke of No.2 led the way, and the rest followed one by one, I think at 2 or 3 minute intervals. In order to avoid any chance of pilots losing their way, he had issued strict orders to No. 2 that they were to fly along the French coast as far as the Somme, and then follow that river up to Amiens; however one of his most dashing pilots, Harvey-Kelly, decided to save time, and cut straight across country from Boulogne to Amiens, thus arriving first and incurring the disciplinary wrath of Burke when he found that he had been beaten in the race.

On the way over to France Maurice Baring had heard both Geoffrey Salmond and Charles Longcroft prophesy that Harvey-Kelly would be the first to land.

The South African connection

Among the small, pioneering, gallant band who flew to France in August 1914 were two unlikely individuals, Second Lieutenants G S Creed and K van der Spuy. In 1913 the South African Government decided to form the nucleus of an aviation corps, as part of the South African Defence Forces. Ten candidates were chosen and some basic flying instruction carried out at a civilian flying school at Kimberley. After the machines had been written off in crashes, six students were selected to finish their training with the RFC in England. Arriving in the spring of 1914 they were posted to the Central Flying School at Upavon in Wiltshire for training. Five of the South Africans qualified and with war clouds gathering they applied for permission from the Union Defence authorities in South Africa to serve with the RFC. This was a constitutional problem as members of the Union Defence Forces were only allowed to serve within South Africa but fortunately consent was given. One of the five, Kenneth van der Spuy, in his autobiography *Chasing the Wind*, wrote about the unusual situation they found themselves in:

Captain Kenneth van der Spuy.

It is a somewhat ironical reflection that a bare fourteen years earlier I had - through Great Britain's action in waging an unfair war against my country - developed an intense hatred against

Britain and everything British. Now, here was I, a member of her corps d'élite, setting forth to do battle for Great Britain against her enemies! I have often since wondered whether - had we been sent to Germany to complete our flying training - we would have volunteered for service with the German Flying Corps; maybe we would have done so.

Despite the bitterness of the Boer War, by the end of the Great War many thousands of South Africans had served and been killed fighting with the British army. And to prove that grudges were not harboured, by 1918 van der Spuy had been awarded an MC, been Mentioned in Despatches and was a Lieutenant Colonel commanding an RAF Wing.

In 1921 he was Chief Staff Officer of the new South African Air Force and during the Second World War was posted to the South African High Commission in London as military adviser. He retired after the war as a Major General, having also been awarded a CBE. He died at the grand age of 99 in 1991.

Again in *Chasing the Wind* he wrote of his landing in France:

On arrival at Amiens, where the bright red Bovril van I had seen at Dover stood out prominently on the edge of the airfield, I made three attempts to land. The aerodrome was surrounded by a large crowd of enthusiastic French, every man, woman and child anxious to shower flowers on and embrace their English compatriots who had arrived to shoot the Bosche out of the sky! Accordingly, every time I attempted to put my wheels on the ground, they surged across the aerodrome like a flock of sheep and it was some time before Major Longcroft of the R.F.C. who was on the ground to receive us, managed - with, literally, whip and abuse - to keep them off! Fortunately, there were no casualties - but there might very easily have been.

Headquarters RFC and the machines of 2, 3 and 4 Squadron moved to Maubeuge on 16 August. They were well supplied with motor transport, having commandeered a motley collection of vehicles from various civilian firms. The transport made them very mobile, which was just as well, with the headlong retreat from Maubeuge only eleven days later. The bright red bomb lorry of 5 Squadron, with the gold legend on its sides - *The World's Favourite Appetiser* - was to be a useful beacon for weary pilots and observers as the RFC retreated from one field to another.

It has proved impossible to discover to what extent Pont-de-Metz was used during the First War. The likelihood is probably very little, considering that in 1916 the French opened the large aerodrome at

110

Cachy, only fifteen kilometres to the east. The aerodrome was probably too small and, in the event, it was abandoned in about 1925 by the Amiens Flying Club.

Return to the Boulevard de Chateaudun via the N29. Turn right and continue along the Boulevard de Chateaudun. The road becomes the Boulevard de Bapaume. After about two kilometres look for a sign on the right to Cimetière St Auchel. Turn right into Rue de 3ème D I or Rue de Cottench (it has two names). The cemetery is on the left.

St Acheul French National Cemetery

The municipal and French National Cemetery are next to each other. In the military cemetery there are 2,739 French, 10 Belgians, 1 Russian and 12 British. The British section is immediately on your left as you enter.

Between the declaration of war and its arrival in France the RFC had already suffered two casualties. Second Lieutenant R R Skene and Airman R K Barlow of 3 Squadron had been killed taking off from Netheravon en-route to Dover. On 16 August the RFC left Amiens for Maubeuge and the dubious historic distinction of the first casualties on active service of not only the RFC, but also the British army, again fell to 3 Squadron. Second Lieutenant Evelyn Walter Copland Perry and Airman Second Class Herbert Edward Parfitt were killed when their BE8 or *Bloater*, as it was known, crashed on take off at Pont-de-Metz.

Perry was another pioneer pilot and had considerable experience. Educated at Repton and Trinity College, Cambridge, he worked at the Royal Aircraft Factory at Farnborough from early 1911 until the middle of 1912. He learned to fly at the Aeronautical Syndicate School of Flying at Brooklands and was awarded his 'ticket', No. 130, on 30 August 1911. While at Farnborough he flew a number of the early experimental machines there, as well as helping Geoffrey de Havilland with his Hydro-Aeroplane. In July 1912 he joined Tommy Sopwith's school at Brooklands, where one of his pupils was Hugh Trenchard (later the first Marshal of the Royal Air Force, Lord Trenchard). Apart from instructing, Perry also participated in air races and air displays. In late 1912 he had demonstrated an Avro 500 biplane to the Portugese and in March 1913 he joined the RFC as a second lieutenant. In partnership with F P H Beadle he designed and built two biplanes, the first of which was later purchased by the Admiralty.

At the Olympia Aero Show in 1914, he and Beadle displayed the

Lieutenant E W C Perry, the first British officer killed on active service in the Great War, on 16 August 1914.

flying boat they had designed, though it had been built by Saunders of Cowes. Despite a number of novel features, it did not prove to be a success. In June 1914 Perry's leg was broken by the starting handle of a car. On the outbreak of war he was declared fit despite still limping from his injury and joined 3 Squadron at Netheravon.

Number 5 Squadron RFC only arrived in France on 15 August due to a number of crashes en-route to Dover from Gosport and also a lack of shipping space for their transport and equipment. One of the pilots, Captain G I Carmichael, later wrote:

The machine I flew over the Channel from Dover to Amiens on 15th August 1914, was a BE8, a type I had not flown before but whose evils I was soon to learn. Petrol to the engine was supplied from a small gravity tank fed by the main tank by a hand pump, but the pump was in the passenger cockpit whilst the pressure gauge was in the cockpit of the pilot and there were no ear phones for inter-communication. I soon found that my passenger was pumping without any word from me and that there was not only risk of starvation but, far worse, excessive pumping, flooding of petrol and fire. However, the fates were kind and although my passenger did not hear a single word from me the whole trip, owing to the noise of the engine and the rush of air on the open cockpits, his guesswork got us safely to our destination.

The BE8, No. 625, which Carmichael flew over was the same machine Perry and Parfitt were flying when they crashed. He later recalled the accident and gave his impressions of the Bloater:

Before I left, there were two tragic accidents, both of BE8s.

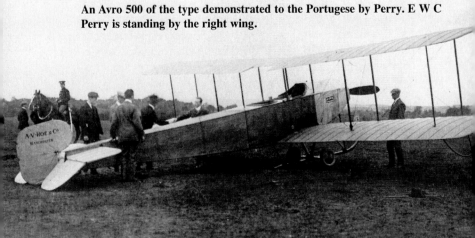

An Avro 500 of the type demonstrated to the Portugese by Perry. E W C Perry is standing by the right wing.

The Perry-Beadle flying boat during tests on Lake Windermere in 1914.

One was that of Copland Parry (sic), whose engine failed getting off; the machine stalled and dived into the ground immediately bursting into flames and although this was within a few yards of myself and others it was impossible to get near enough to drag the occupants from the fierce flames and both perished. Shortly after, Smith Barry with his mechanic also stalled his machine which spun into the ground but, fortunately, it did not burst into flames though the mechanic was killed and Smith Barry broke his leg. The cause of both accidents, spinning, was the inadequate fin surface of the small vertical plane immediately in front of the rudder which allowed the tail of the machine to swing round the nose if a turn was attempted with too much rudder and not enough bank of the wings.

After this further tragic evidence of the evil character of the BE8, I so disliked it that I had no desire to fly that type again. Of all the thirty and more machines that I piloted in the Service, I can only recount three that I distrusted or disliked and the BE8

BE8 625, the machine that Perry and Parfitt were flying when they were killed on 16 August 1914.

was one of them.

The details of Perry's life are comprehensive but very little is known about Parfitt who, like most other ranks in the British forces, seems to have been regarded as a second class citizen. A native of Croydon, he had joined the RFC in May 1913 with a service number of 725 and was 21 years old when he was killed.

The funeral was held the following day and was an impressive affair. The flag-covered carriages were escorted by several senior officers and troops from the Welsh Fusiliers, as well as a contingent of French troops. The streets were lined with the local populace and all members of the RFC attended.

As the first casualties suffered by the British army on active service in the First World War and the first ever by the RFC, the inscription on Perry's headstone is poignant: *First on the Roll of Honour; all glory to his name.*

For more information about Perry and Parfitt there is an excellent article on the RFC's early casualties entitled *First Names on the Roll of Honour* by Jeff Taylor in *Cross and Cockade International*, Volume 23.

Return to the Boulevard de Bapaume and turn right along it. Turn right onto the D934 signposted to Longeau. Proceed straight through Longeau on the D934. After approximately five kilometres turn left on the D168 to Gentelles and then on to the village of Cachy. As you enter Cachy village there is a concrete block barn on the right and a corrugated iron barn set back on your left. Turn left down the gravel track to the left of the barn and halt at the T-junction. In the distance to the north are the trees of Bois l'Abbé.

Cachy Aerodrome

This site is of importance for two reasons. It was here that the first *Groupes de Combat* in the French air service were formed in October 1916. Also the famous *Lafayette Escadrille* served here from October 1916 until January 1917.

The *Groupes de Combat*

On 21 February 1916 the German army launched its offensive against the French at Verdun. The Germans knew that the French would defend the city to the last man and therefore were intending to suck in and then bleed the French army to death. Initially the French Air Service found itself at both a numerical and tactical disadvantage. The commander of the V *Armée* aviation element, *Commandant* Charles de Tricornet de Rose was given authority to assemble whatever resources he needed to remedy the situation. He requested all available Morane and Nieuport fighters, plus some of the best pilots from other units, and grouped them together. By flying continuous patrols this *Groupe de Chasse* gradually wrested aerial superiority from the Germans.

At the end of July 1916 the Allies launched their offensive on the Somme, partly to draw some of the German resources away from Verdun and thus relieve the pressure on the French. Though primarily a British affair, the bloody Battle of the Somme involved the French VI *Armée*, who were south of them on their right flank.

Prior to the battle the French, with their experience at Verdun, increased their fighter strength by posting in several *escadrilles* equipped with Nieuport scouts. The French already had one unit, *N*103, at Cachy, southeast of Amiens, but reinforced it with *N*3, *N*26, *N*37, *N*62, *N*65, *N*67, and *N*73. The *N* prefix denoted the squadrons were equipped with Nieuports and when they later re-equipped with Spads this changed to *Spa*. This grouping of units was designated *Groupement de Combat de la Somme* and was commanded by *Capitaine* Felix Brocard, the CO of *N*3.

Many of the top French aces, such as Jean Navarre, Charles Nungesser, René Dorme, Georges Guynemer and Albert Deullin were based at Cachy during the Somme battle in the summer of 1916. Between mid-April and the end of October 1916 the units at Cachy claimed fifty-two German machines.

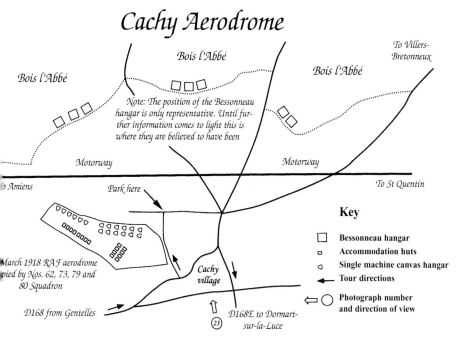

Cachy Aerodrome

Bois l'Abbé

Bois l'Abbé

Bois l'Abbé

Bois l'Abbé

To Villers-Bretonneux

Note: The position of the Bessonneau hangar is only representative. Until further information comes to light this is where they are believed to have been

Motorway

Motorway

b Amiens

Park here

To St Quentin

March 1918 RAF aerodrome pied by Nos. 62, 73, 79 and 80 Squadron

Cachy village

D168 from Gentelles

D168E to Dommart-sur-la-Luce

(23)

Key

☐ Bessonneau hangar

▫ Accommodation huts

◁ Single machine canvas hangar

◄── Tour directions

⇐ ○ Photograph number and direction of view

Picture No. 23. Cachy aerodrome looking across the village in a north westerly direction at the Bois l'Abbé.

Nieuport scouts of *Escadrille N*103 at Cachy in October 1916. They were the first unit based at Cachy.

General Duval, with *Capitaine* Brocard, inspecting pilots of *Groupement de Combat de la Somme* at Cachy in June 1916. Through the gap, behind the General, can be seen Georges Guynemer, the most successful pilot in the *Groupement*.

Albert Deullin photographed at Cachy. He scored ten victories while with *Escadrille N*3 and later commanded *N*73 and *GC* 18. Note the dark Stork emblem on his machine.

Groupe de Combat 12, les Cignones

In October 1916 the grouping of fighter *escadrilles* was formalised by the official establishment of *Groupes de Combat*. The first three were *GC*11, *GC*12 and *GC*13 and of these *Groupes*, *GC* 12 and *GC*13, were based at Cachy.

Groupe de Combat 12 was commanded by Felix Brocard, who had led *Escadrille N3*, and consisted of *Escadrilles N3*, *N26*, *N73* and *N103*. Though the official designation of these *escadrilles* was *GC*12 it was more popularly known as *Les Cigognes* or the Storks after the emblem decorating their machines. *N3* had been the first unit to employ this marking as they had been formed at Belfort in Alsace and the stork is the traditional symbol for the region. Each *Escadrille* had a slightly different style of stork on their machines.

Brocard, born in 1885, was a career officer and had entered the Military School at St Cyr in 1905. He had been commissioned into the infantry in 1907 and had then learned to fly in 1911, receiving his French Aero Club brevet, No. 123, in February 1912. He was promoted to command *MS* 3 in March 1915. (*MS3* were equipped with Morane-Saulnier machines and the change in designation to *N3* occurred on their re-equipment with Nieuport aeroplanes). Brocard scored the unit's first victory on 3 July 1915.

The first pilot to score five confirmed victories in *N3* was Georges Guynemer. (See *Airfields and Airmen: Ypres* page 142 for an account of Guynemer's career.) By the time of the formation of *GC*12 Guynemer was the *escadrille's* most successful pilot with eighteen victories. By the time of his death on 11 September 1917, he had shot down fifty-three enemy aircraft.

The first victory for *GC*12 was scored on 1 November 1916, by Lieutenant Armand Pinsard of *N26*. He also had been a pre-war soldier and had learned to fly in 1912. Early in the war he had been forced to land in enemy territory and been taken prisoner of war but had managed to escape. He served again during the Second World War, being badly wounded and losing a leg. Pinsard died in 1953.

During the autumn of 1916 the *Groupe* claimed approximately forty enemy machines, despite the frequently poor weather. By the time that they left Cachy Guynemer had scored thirty victories, Nungesser twenty one and Dorme seventeen.

With the end of the Somme offensive and the onset of winter, enemy activity decreased considerably. Between 23 and 29 January 1917, *Les Cignones* moved to Manoncourt-en-Vermois in the French VIII *Armée* sector.

The hangars of *Escadrille N65* at Cachy in the bitter winter of 1916/1917.

By the end of the war *GC*12 had claimed 291 German aeroplanes and balloons. One of its members, René Fonck, had become the French and Allied leading ace with seventy-five victories. The unit fought again during the Second World War and after the fall of France continued in North Africa. It finished the war as part of the RAF and is still serving in the *L'Armée de l'Air*. (See *The Storks* by Frank Bailey and Norman Franks for an excellent history of *Groupe de Combat* 12.)

The *Lafayette Escadrille*

The other *Groupe de Combat* at Cachy, *GC*13, comprised *Escadrilles N*65, *N*67, *N*112 and *N*124. The last formation, *N*124, though commanded by a Frenchman, *Capitaine* Georges Thenault, consisted mainly of Americans who had volunteered for service with the French long before their own country came in to the war. They were known more popularly as the *Lafayette Escadrille* or *Escadrille Américaine* and had officially formed in April 1916. In October they moved from their well-appointed aerodrome at Luxeuil, only eighty kilometres from the Swiss border, to the canvas hangars and huts on the windswept plateau at Cachy.

The *Lafayette* had in its ranks many colourful individuals, some of whom had served in the French Foreign Legion. The unit also had interesting pets and had two lion cubs christened Whiskey and Soda.

Ted Parsons, in his entertaining autobiography *I Flew with the Lafayette Escadrille* wrote of the conditions at Cachy thus:

> *In place of luxurious villas and tasty, well-cooked hotel food, the escadrille was assigned with five other French escadrilles to portable barracks, erected in a sea of mud. Cold and damp fog penetrated every crack and crevice, and these big sheds were anything but watertight. There were no arrangements for*

119

Whiskey and Soda. Whiskey was blind in one eye as a result of a blow to the head. When they became too large they were given to a Paris zoo.

cooking, and for some time the boys had to depend on the hospitality of the other squadrons, who generously saw that no one went hungry. There weren't enough blankets and everyone had to sleep in his fur-lined flying suit.

In desperation, many nights I slept with Whiskey, taking him to bed with me to try to keep me warm. Anyone who has never tried sleeping on a folding canvas camp bed with a half-grown lion has a neat thrill in prospect. From my point of view, it wasn't an unqualified success. I always put him down at the foot in an endeavour to keep my feet from freezing, but sometime during the night he'd work his way up, and I'd awake in the cold grey light using him for a pillow and my mouth full of evil-tasting lion fur. I guess perhaps lions aren't supposed to smell like the perfumes of Araby. In any event, Whiskey smelled pretty awful. He wasn't any too careful about his bathing or personal hygiene, and in addition, he had a remarkably well-developed case of halitosis. Still, I couldn't complain, for a lion should smell like a lion, and he did help wonderfully to keep me from freezing.

Conditions were not improved by the attentions of German night bombers intent on disrupting Allied supply lines and aerodromes, as Parsons continues:

On December 9 the Boche came over and dropped eight bombs on the camp at Cachy. One of the bombs made a direct hit on the hangar of the N-3, the famous Stork escadrille of the heroic Captain Guynemer, which was located just beside that of our escadrille.

The hangar, fed by the gasoline from the wrecked ships, blazes up in a hurry, and one of the mechanics was burned to death. He was pinned under a plane knocked over by the explosion of the bomb. When the rescue squad got him out, in his charred hand was found a knife with which he had desperately tried to cut himself free.

It was a bitterly cold night, and the boys had hurriedly thrown on what warm clothes they could find at the first warning of the raiding planes. The German ships continued to circle overhead, dropping bombs all around the light of the blazing hangar. The ground was alive with running, shouting figures trying to save the planes in the other hangars, despite a merciless barrage of machine-gun fire from the low-flying bombers.

In the two-volume history of the *Lafayette* entitled *The Lafayette Flying Corps*, edited by James Norman Hall and Charles Bernard Nordhoff, there is a further insight in to the conditions at Cachy:

Something had to be done, so Thaw and Masson, who is our Chef de Popote (President of the Mess), obtained permission to go to Paris in one of our light trucks. They returned with cooking-utensils, a stove, and other necessary things. All hands set to work, and as a result life was made bearable. In fact I was surprised to find the quarters as good as they were when I rejoined the escadrille a couple of weeks after its arrival on the Somme. Outside of the cold, mud, and dampness, it wasn't so bad. The barracks had been partitioned off into little rooms leaving a large space for a dining-hall. The stove was set up there, and all animated life from the lion cub to the pilots centred around it.

The eight escadrilles of fighting machines formed an interesting colony. The large canvas hangars were surrounded by the house tents of their respective escadrilles; wooden barracks for the men and pilots were in close proximity, and between the encampments of the various units were the tents of the commanding officers. In addition there was a bath-house and the power plant which generated electric light for the tents and barracks; and in one very popular tent was the community bar, the profits from which were sent to the Red Cross.

We had never before been grouped with so many combat squadrons, nor at a field so near the Front. We sensed the war to better advantage than at Luxeil or Bar-le-Duc. When there is activity on the lines, the rumble of heavy artillery reaches us in a heavy volume of sound. From the field one can see the line of observation balloons, and beyond them distant patrols, darting like swallows in the shrapnel puffs of anti-aircraft fire. The roar

121

of motors that are being tested is punctuated by the staccato barking of machine guns, and at intervals the hollow, whistling sound of a fast plane diving to earth is added to this symphony of war notes.

Cachy, like a lot of aerodromes was probably more than one field, especially considering eight *escadrilles* were based there. Despite much research it has proved impossible to locate exactly where the huts and hangars were, though it is almost certain that they were in the trees at the southern edge of the Bois l'Abbé. The RFC had a temporary aerodrome in March 1918 to the west of the village where Nos. 62, 73, 79 and 80 Squadrons were based before this site became too close to the front line and was abandoned. The village of Cachy was destroyed in the fighting of 1918, though later rebuilt in a similar layout.

Return to the road through the village and turn left. After the church turn right along the D523 and D168E to Domart-sur-la-Luce. Turn left along the D934 for a short distance and then turn left on the D76 to Hangard. The cemetery is a short distance beyond the village centre.

Hangard Communal Cemetery Extension

At the end of March 1918 the front line ran through Hangard and it was the scene of bitter fighting, as the Allies tried to prevent the German army breaking through to Amiens.

The extension to the cemetery (19/3) originally had only 51 graves, of which nineteen were German. Casualties were concentrated here from over a dozen other cemeteries, including a number of German ones that no longer exist, until the burials now number over 550.

Welinkar lies at the very back of the cemetery against the wall to the left of the seat. The first time I came here the roses were absolutely beautiful - a credit to the War Graves Commission gardeners.

Shri Krishna Chunda Welinkar (III J1)

Very few Indians seem to have served in the RFC/RAF as pilots, of whom two were killed and one taken prisoner of war.

Welinkar, born on 24 October 1894,was the son of Mrs. Lakshmibai or Lucy Welinkar of Ridge Road, Shri Krishna Niwas, Bombay, though she also gave her address as The Palace, Gwalior. His sister-in-law was Her Highness, The Princess Tihare.

There is an element of doubt as to his nationality, as he was described at various times as English or Indian, though his father seems to have been British. A well educated man, who spoke Persian, Arabic and Hindustani, he was a student at Jesus College, Oxford, studying History and Law in 1916.

He learned to fly at the Grahame-White School at Hendon on a Grahame-White biplane and obtained his Royal Aero Club certificate, No. 3327, on 10 August 1916. He then attempted to join the RFC but met the official stance that only English or naturalised Englishmen were eligible for a commission and it was recommended that he become an air mechanic. While trying to enter the RFC he joined the Oxfordshire and Buckinghamshire Light Infantry in the ranks on 13 February 1917. Eventually he was granted a commission in the RFC by Brigadier-General Sefton Brancker.

Shri Krishna Chunda Welinkar, 23 Squadron RAF.

After joining the RFC he did his initial training at Oxford before undertaking flying training with 3 Reserve Squadron at Shoreham and 19 Training Squadron at Hounslow.

Unfortunately his training was delayed by two serious accidents. On 13 August 1917, while with 65 Squadron at Wye, he lost his engine on take off and spun his Camel into the ground from fifty feet. He regained consciousness after six hours in Ashford VAD Hospital and spent a week in hospital with a damaged knee.

Advanced training was with 87 Squadron at Joyce Green, near Dartford, on the Thames estuary, but he was involved in yet another serious accident. On 11 November 1917, he was airborne for his first solo in a De Havilland DH5. Turning down wind at 400 feet, the nose went down and he just cleared a bank before hitting the ground without flattening out. Unconscious for four hours, he was admitted to No. 3 Australian Auxiliary Hospital at Dartford with a broken right arm and facial injuries. He was then transferred to the RFC Hospital in Bryanston Square in London, where he had an operation on his damaged nose on 17 December.

At his medical board in London on 28 January 1918, it was recommended that he remain in the UK for another three to four weeks and not fly above 12,000 feet. In fact he had flown five hours since his accident and reached that altitude already.

At long last he received his operational posting and arrived at 23 Squadron, who were based at Bertangles, on 10 April 1918. The squadron was in the process of exchanging its French built Spads for Sopwith Dolphins.

The Sopwith Dolphin

The designer of the Dolphin, Herbert Smith, intended that the pilot should have the best view possible and to this end he put the upper wing level with the pilot's eyes. The result of this configuration meant he had to put back stagger on the wings, thus giving the machine a rather odd look. With his head sticking through the wing centre section cutout the pilot had an unrivalled view, though there was some concern as to what would happen if the machine turned over on the ground. The Dolphin had an excellent performance and was well liked by its pilots. It was very much an underrated machine, being in some respects a better aeroplane than the SE5a. The first examples were delivered to 19 Squadron in December 1917 and 23 Squadron, the third unit to receive them, were fully re-equipped by the first week in May. Sadly only two other squadrons, Nos.79 and 87, were to employ the Dolphin before the war ended.

The official 23 Squadron badge. Motto: Semper Aggressus (Always on the Attack).

Welinkar departed Bertangles at 0945 hours on 27 June 1918, for an Offensive Patrol and was last seen low down in combat with a two-seater near Peronne. His failure to return generated considerable correspondence for the Casualty department at the Air Ministry, which was still flying back and forth in early 1919. There was some confusion as to whether he was a prisoner of war or had been killed. In a casualty list dropped over the Allied lines by the Germans his name had been

Sopwith Dolphin D5315 'K' of 23 Squadron on the aerodrome at Foucaucourt in August 1918. The white disc was the squadron's marking. Note the back stagger of the wings and the narrow gap between the fuselage and the upper wing.

Te... No.: REGENT 8000.
Telegraphic Address: "AIRMINISTRY, LONDON."
(All   rams on the subject of this letter, should
  q   the undermentioned Air Ministry Refce.)

HAC/MRJ.

AIR MINISTRY,

STRAND,

LONDON, W.C.2.

1st January 1919.

All letters on the undermentioned subject should be addressed to THE SECRETARY at the above address and should quote :

Air Ministry Refce. P.2.Cas.   Your Refce.

SUBJECT :—

Major E.J.Briscoe,
    Royal Air Force
        Headquarters,
            BRITISH EXPEDITIONARY FORCE
                FRANCE.

My dear Briscoe,

Lieut.S.K.C.WELINKAR.

   We continue to be inundated from every quarter with enquiries in regard to this Officer.   The latest is a telegram from Simla, the copy of which I send you.   Will you please take this up with Captain M. Pye-Smith, as we do not know of any list which has been circulated by your Headquarters, in any case such has not been transmitted here.

   The latest I have is that the Officer is supposed to have been buried in Rouvroy and I have taken this up with the Geneva Red Cross who reported it, to find out which Rouvroy it is, so far without result.

   If you could locate his grave I should be deeply grateful.

Yours sincerely,

[signature]

A slightly exasperated letter from the Air Ministry casualty department, P.2.Cas. , concerning Welinkar's disappearance.

misspelt and the RAF did not feel that this was sufficient proof officially to declare him killed in action. In fact he had been shot down and had died three days later in an enemy field hospital, after suffering a fractured leg below the knee from a gunshot wound. There was also some doubt as to where he was buried, but today he lies in the quiet of Hangard, thousands of miles away from his homeland. The inscription on his headstone reads: *To the honoured memory of one of the Empire's bravest sons who made the great sacrifice.*

Continue ahead on the D76 until you meet the D23. Turn left along the D23 until you have passed Crucifix Corner Cemetery on your left and driven over the bridge of the new Amiens to St Quentin motorway. Stop just after the bridge and before reaching the large farm on the left.

Villers-Bretonneux Aerodrome 1915

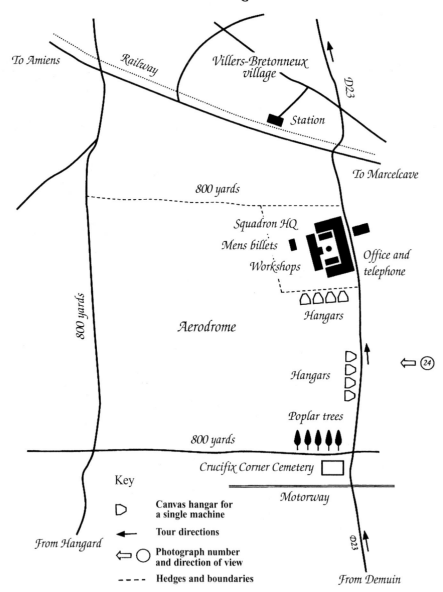

To Amiens

Railway

Villers-Bretonneux
village

D23

Station

To Marcelcave

800 yards

Squadron HQ

Mens billets

Workshops

Office and
telephone

Hangars

800 yards

Aerodrome

Hangars

⇐ (24)

Poplar trees

800 yards

Crucifix Corner Cemetery

Motorway

From Hangard

D23

From Demuin

Key

▷   Canvas hangar for
a single machine

◀   Tour directions

⇐ ○   Photograph number
and direction of view

- - - -   Hedges and boundaries

Picture No. 24. Villers-Bretonneux 1915 aerodrome looking west.

Number 11 Squadron

The field on your left is the 1915 Villers-Bretonneux aerodrome and the farm, La Couture, was used as squadron offices.

Number 11 Squadron RFC was based here for little more than five weeks before moving to Bertangles and seems to have been the only unit to utilise the field. The aerodrome then appears to have been abandoned for reasons unknown. The Villers-Bretonneux aerodrome in use from early 1917 until abandoned in the March 1918 German advance was east of the village. The whole area was devastated in 1918 and the present farm on the 1915 site is of a similar size but a different layout, as one can see by comparing the present day photograph of the buildings with the aerodrome diagram.

The 11 Squadron crest. Motto: Ociores Acrioresque Aquilis (Swifter and Keener than Eagles).

On 20 September 1915 No. 11 Squadron moved from Vert Galand to the new airfield. A J Insall in *Observer* wrote:

> It so happened that we were on the eve of an entire move to a new aerodrome south of the Somme, at a place called Villers-Bretonneux, where for some days past a party of British civilian craftsmen sent out from this country had been erecting wooden hangars for our use.

Lionel Rees

Most of the squadron moved to the new aerodrome, but Insall and other members of B Flight went north to strengthen units about to be engaged in the Battle of Loos. One of the 11 Squadron personnel who went to Villers-Bretonneux or Villers-Bret, as the squadron called it, was the redoubtable Lionel Rees. Insall wrote of Rees:

Captain Rees was one of those rare men who are born leaders, who never flap, and who believe essentially in precept - and who never despise the novice. Rees it was, also, who taught us in No.11 Squadron that our cardinal rule of behaviour on the battlefront must always adhere to the Flying Corp's watch-word: 'Go in to the attack! - Whenever you see a Hun, no matter where he is, be he alone or accompanied, go for him, and shoot him down...'

Of commanding appearance and stature, possessed, I should say, of the most captivating eye-twinkle of any officer whom I can recall, Rees was respected and liked by all those who came into contact with him. I was never in his flight, and yet I never passed him by without receiving some smiling acknowledgement of my existence.

It was Rees who was the pilot of the Vickers that accounted for the first enemy machine to be shot down, on our side of the lines, by our squadron.

The machine, of course, was that flown by Fritz Kölpin and Ernst Leonhardi of *FA* 23, who now lie in Forceville Military Cemetery - the last entry of the previous chapter. They fell victim to Rees ten days after the arrival at Villers-Bretonneux. As noted in the Forceville Cemetery Rees and Hargreaves were decorated for this action and other good work.

James McKinley Hargreaves DCM

Rees was awarded the MC and Hargreaves received the Distinguished Conduct Medal. This was a comparatively rare decoration for the RFC/RAF, in that just under 100 were awarded, including only one Bar (6391 Corporal/ Acting Sergeant F Johnson). This is a small number, considering that between 1914 and 1920 about 25,000 DCMs were awarded, with another 5,000 made available to our Allies. Of the total of nearly 100 air awards, less than half were for aerial action, the others being for work on the ground or general awards.

Hargreaves' DCM citation read:

For conspicuous gallantry and skill on several occasions, notably the following:-

On 21st September, 1915, when in a machine armed with one machine-gun and piloted by Captain Rees, a large German

Biplane armed with two machine-guns was sighted 2,000 feet below. Our machine spiralled down and engaged the enemy, who, being faster, manoeuvred to get broadside on and then opened fire. The attack, however, was pressed, and the engine of the enemy's biplane was apparently struck, for after a quick turn it glided down some distance and then fell just inside the German lines. On 31st August Captain Rees, with Flight-Serjeant Hargreaves, fought a powerful German machine for three-quarters of an hour. They then returned for more ammunition and went out again to the attack. Finally the enemy's machine was brought down and apparently wrecked.

Flight Sergeant J M Hargreaves DCM of 11 Squadron.

James McKinlay Hargreaves was older than most of his contemporaries, having been born in Glasgow on 19 January 1883. He enlisted in the Royal Scots on 24 May 1905, having previously been a labourer. By October 1912 he had reached the rank of sergeant and spent five years with his regiment in India. In fact two of his six children were born there. Returning from India in April 1914, he transferred to the RFC the following month. In March 1915 Hargreaves received promotion to Flight Sergeant.

Flying training in the First World War was unbelievably rapid. Just two weeks after the fight with Kölpin and Leonhardi, Hargreaves qualified as a pilot, receiving Royal Aero Club certificate number 1887 on 13 October 1915! At this stage of the war the RFC had a flying school at Le Crotoy, on the mouth of the river Somme, and pilots learned to fly without returning to Home Establishment.

Promoted to temporary Sergeant Major, in May 1916 he was serving with 32 Squadron at Netheravon, where he re-engaged in order to complete 21 years service. From May 1916 until March 1917, he was once again in France, but whether this was with 32 Squadron is not known. Whether he flew as a pilot in France is also unknown. On 30 May 1917 he was discharged as being no longer physically fit for service.

Continue north on the D23 into the village of Villers-Bretonneux. Turn right onto the N29. Shortly after leaving the village there will be a sign to the right to an industrial zone. Further along the road there is a turning to the right, the C203. The aerodrome was on the south of the N29 and between these two points.

Villers-Bretonneux Aerodrome 1917

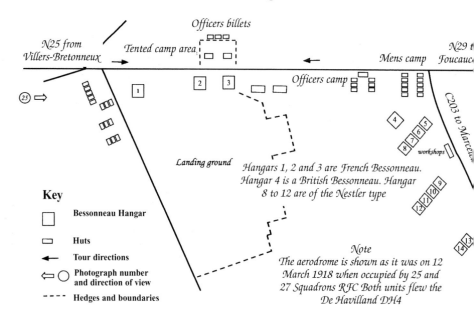

Officers billets

N25 from Villers-Bretonneux

Tented camp area

N29 t Foucauc

Mens camp

Officers camp

(25)

1

2   3

Officers camp

4

5
6
7
8   workshops

9
10
11
12

13
14

C203 to Marcel

Landing ground

Hangars 1, 2 and 3 are French Bessonneau. Hangar 4 is a British Bessonneau. Hangar 8 to 12 are of the Nestler type

Key

☐ Bessonneau Hangar

▭ Huts

← Tour directions

⇐ ○ Photograph number and direction of view

- - - - Hedges and boundaries

Note
The aerodrome is shown as it was on 12 March 1918 when occupied by 25 and 27 Squadrons RFC Both units flew the De Havilland DH4

This aerodrome was one of a number that the French handed over to the RFC as the British extended their line and they very generously left all the hangars and huts behind. At this time the RFC was short of accommodation and the donation of the Bessonneaux hangars was very useful and much appreciated. The aerodrome, by First World War standards, was very large and comprised two fields, to the south of the

Picture No. 25. Villers-Bretonneux 1917 aerodrome looking due east.

SITE OF AERODROME

Nieuport scout of *N*3 at Villers-Bretonneux in October 1916. This was the machine of *Capitaine* Alfred Auger, who later commanded the unit. He was killed in action on 28 July 1917. Note the different style of Stork on the fuselage.

Villers-Bretonneux to St Quentin road. If you drive along this very straight Roman road eastward, it is virtually a plain, with only the gentlest of undulations and at any spot along this highway could be placed a large airfield. Between January 1917 and March 1918, when it was abandoned, Villers-Bretonneux was home to Nos. 24, 25, 27, 34 and 35 Squadrons RFC.

Maurice Baring in *Flying Corps Headquarters 1914 - 1918* wrote of a visit he and Trenchard made to the French aerodromes at Cachy and Villers-Bretonneux:

> *On the 20th of September, 1916, I went with the General to see a crack French Squadron at Cachi (sic). There we saw Guynemer, the famous French pilot, who looked like a young eagle. The General presented Commandant Pugo with his D.S.O. and from there we went on to another French Aerodrome at Villers-Bretonneux. While we were there in the office a young observer arrived straight from an artillery shoot, and marked in the line on the map. The General was immensely impressed with the precision and straightforwardness of his work, as he also was with the whole organisation of the French photography and registration.*

Continue along the N29 for a short distance and turn left on the C201 to Hamel. From Hamel follow the D71 and after less than one kilometre turn left on the C7 to Bouzencourt. Just before the village on the left is a memorial flanked by two Scots Pines and a maple tree.

The memorial to Mond and Martyn.

F L Mond and E M Martyn

There are very few flying memorials on the Western Front, for the RFC Brigade and Wing system did not seem to lend itself to this sort of commemoration in the same way as the army divisional system. The loyalty of aircrew was to their squadron, and Brigade Headquarters was a vague administrative centre miles away that the average airman probably never saw. In addition squadrons were frequently moved from one wing to another.

This memorial is a traditional broken column, symbolising the abrupt cutting off of a life in its prime. The column is showing the effects and ravages of time and the inscription is now difficult to read. However, it is well cared for by the local people and has been repaired a number of times.

The De Havilland DH 4

The DH4 first flew in August 1916 with Geoffrey de Havilland at the controls and was to be one of the great designs of the war. The superb Rolls-Royce Eagle engine gave the DH 4 an excellent performance, though delays in engine deliveries also affected the rate and numbers of DH 4s arriving in squadrons. The first DH 4s received by 57 Squadron arrived in May 1917, replacing their ageing FE2ds. The performance of the machine meant it could be used for day bombing and it was on such a mission that F L Mond and E M Martyn were killed.

Just after nine o'clock on the morning of 15 May 1918, twelve machines lifted off from 57 Squadron's aerodrome at Le Quesnoy, just north of Abbeville, to bomb enemy supply dumps around Bapaume. Two machines, in addition to dropping bombs, were also designated to take photographs of the operation. Over 100 25 pound bombs were dropped on the target but two machines failed to return, with all four crew members being killed.

Francis Leopold Mond was born in 1896 and came from Storrington in Sussex. He had served in the London Division Ammunition Column of the Royal Field Artillery and then joined the RFC in early 1915. After pilot training at Brooklands, Farnborough and Hounslow he had served in France for four months with an unknown unit (possibly 16 Squadron). On his return to England he served with two squadrons working up for service overseas, and then joined 57 Squadron at Ste Marie-Cappel, west of Ypres. Two days after his arrival the squadron moved down south to Le Quesnoy.

Mond's observer, Edgar Meath Martyn, was a Canadian and had been born on 28 October 1892. After service with the 19th Canadians, he had joined the RFC at the beginning of 1918. Following training at No. 1 School of Aerial Gunnery he reported for duty with 57 Squadron on 18 April 1918, and was to last barely a month. Martyn had been employed as a railway contractor before joining up and had a wife in North Bay, Ontario.

Lieutenant Francis Mond, the pilot of DH4 A7645 lost on 15 May 1918

They were seen in combat with three enemy machines and their aeroplane crashed at Bouzencourt, near Corbie. They probably fell victim to *Leutnant* Johann Janzen, commanding officer of *Jasta* 6. The wreckage fell between the British and German lines and was abandoned as unsalvageable. Their bodies were retrieved by Australian infantry but the location of their graves was subsequently lost.

Mond's mother, after considerable effort and persistence, was able to identify the body of her son and his observer in 1923, at Doullens Communal Cemetery Extension No. 2. Why they are buried over 30 kilometres away from where they crashed is not known. Mond's mother bought the land at the crash site and had a memorial erected. The family visited the monument regularly until the 1950s but by the late 1970s it was in a poor state. The CWGC were unable to trace the family and the responsibility for its maintenance was accepted by the

DH4 A7645 in which Mond and Martyn were lost, involved in a minor accident prior to their fatal flight.

Commune of Hamel. The site is well kept and a credit to the local people. (For more information on this fascinating story see *Private Memorials of the Great War on the Western Front* by Barrie Thorpe.)

The crew from the other machine lost this day, Lieutenant E H Piper and Second Lieutenant H L B Crabbe, are buried or commemorated at Carnoy Military Cemetery. (See the Carnoy Cemetery entry in the next chapter.)

Return to the N29 via the C7, D71 and C201. Turn right along the N29 towards Villers-Bretonneux. In Villers-Bretonneux turn right onto the D23 and continue on this to the cemetery which is on the right.

Villers-Bretonneux Military Cemetery and the Australian National Memorial

This area was the scene of bitter fighting in the spring of 1918 as the Allies tried to prevent the German onslaught from bursting through and taking the vital town of Amiens. On the night of 25 April 1918, a desperate Allied counter attack was mounted by a scratch force which included two brigades from the Australian 5th Division. There was no preliminary artillery barrage and in the fighting that night most of the ground lost the previous day was recovered. A new front line was established and the enemy prevented from taking Amiens.

The cemetery (9/123) is a concentration one, in that bodies were brought here after the war from all over the battlefield and now contains over 2,000 casualties. The impressive structure at the back is the Australian National Memorial for all the Australian dead of the Western Front and most of the men with unknown graves. From the top of the tower there is a magnificent view of the whole area and you can see why the hill was of such strategic importance. The tower has a number of scars inflicted by machine gun fire during the Second World War, when it was used as an observation point. On each Anzac Day, 25 April, there is a parade. Among the more than 2,000 graves are over thirty Great War fliers.

The RAF casualties to whom we have come to pay our respects are in Plot XV1A, which is approximately three-quarters of the way down on the right side beyond the Cross of Sacrifice.

The bombing of Bertangles

The casualties are Second Lieutenant Alexander Urinowski 48 Squadron (XV1A A1), Second Lieutenant James Bruce Jameson, 48

134

Squadron (XVIA C17), Private Patrick Docherty, 85 Squadron (XV1A C18), Airman Second Class Adam Mann, 85 Squadron (XV1A C19) and Airman First Class Leonard Pole, 23 Squadron (XV1A C21). They were all killed in a bombing raid on the aerodrome at Bertangles on 24 August 1918. The 24 Squadron diarist noted:

August 24th. - Exit poor old 48 Squadron!! Just after dinner the Hun made a good shot with a bomb, setting their middle hangar on fire and lighting up the whole place for the remaining Huns, who burnt out all 48 hangars and melted their transport and engines down; the stray bombs destroyed most of 23 Squadron's machines, destroyed 84's middle hangar, and made a few holes in our machines. The Wing offices were well 'ventilated' with splinters, and 23 chickens all went up in a puff of smoke and feathers

The Colonel and I were dining at 46 Squadron, which turned out to be the best place to be. A concert party was in progress in 48 Squadron, and the concert room was about the only place that did not get a direct hit, though the Hun shot them up with machine guns as they came out on the aerodrome. About 50 casualties all told.

Number 48 Squadron, who operated Bristol Fighters, was commanded by Major Keith Park, a New Zealander. During the Battle of Britain he commanded 11 Group, Fighter Command and retired from the RAF as Air Chief Marshal Sir Keith Park GCB, KBE, MC, DFC. He died on 5 February 1975. When at Staff College in the 1920s he wrote of his experiences that night:

Enemy night bombing became more frequent as the summer advanced, and every clear night his machines passed overhead on their way to the coast. When in August Bertangles received attention there were very fortunately only four squadrons in occupation - earlier there had been eight. In July I had commenced sandbagging hangars and quarters and completed this work early in August.

During the first week in the latter month bombs fell near my hangars on two occasions, no casualties being caused.

On the evening of the 25th August the enemy carried out a pre-arranged bomb raid on our aerodrome putting my squadron out of action.

At about 2100 hours the first E.A. crossed the aerodrome at between 6,000 and 7,000 feet, dropping three bombs. The first fell and detonated in a hangar containing six Bristols fully

*loaded with petrol, ammunition, and 25-lb bombs - the second
and third exploded in the centre of the aerodrome.*

*Immediately the hangar burst into flame and well illuminated
the squadron's camp, hangars etc.*

*The first machine circled and unloaded the balance of its load
of bombs, hitting another hangar full of machines and the
transport lines. Between the two hangars hit was one which I had
for some time been using for the station or Wing cinema and
concert hall. This hangar was protected by a sandbag wall four
feet high, and as all the occupants remained seated no one was
hit by flying splinters from the first or second salvo of bombs. As
the 200 (or may have been 250) officers and men streamed out
into the aerodrome the second bomber was heard approaching.
This, coupled with the intense heat of the burning hangars on
either side, caused a complete panic.*

*Stupidly the crowd stampeded towards the approaching
machine, and a number of men were hit by two bombs which fell
short.*

*Before the panic stricken crowd (mostly visitors) got clear of
the camp a bomb fell in its midst killing several officers and
wounding others, also setting the quarters alight.*

*Assisted by my E.O. and a number of Australian privates
bivouacked on the edge of the aerodrome, I managed to drag
seven machines clear of the burning hangars; all were now on
fire.*

*Whilst attempting to get machines into the open the third and
fourth bombers dropped more bombs on the hangars and camp,
wounding several of the small rescue party. In all the bombers
secured thirteen direct hits on hangars, quarters, transport,
offices and workshops.*

*Fortunately the bombs were small ones or our casualty roll
would have been very big.*

*The squadron's losses (below) were light compared with those
amongst visitors and passers by, many being wounded by
splinters -*

*2 officers killed
7 officers wounded
7 O.ranks wounded (?2 killed)*

The casualties amongst visitors were 6 killed and 14

wounded.

All transport was destroyed.

Seven or eight Bristols were rescued, but these were mostly damaged and unserviceable.

The effect on everyone's nerves was very marked for some months later, and I had none of my previous difficulty in getting people to build earth walls round quarters and hangars.

After the above the efficiency of the other ranks fell, as also did that of many of my officers, and the month of September was full of up-hill work. Unluckily, Boisdinghem, where we moved for rest, was on the route used nightly by enemy bombers proceeding to and fro from the coast. The squadron's nerves grew steady at a slow pace even here.

If the concert hall had been hit it would have been a disaster, not only for the squadrons but probably for the Royal Air Force twenty-five years later. In addition to Park, at the concert there was Sholto Douglas, the CO of 84 Squadron (later Marshal of the RAF Lord Douglas of Kirtleside GCB, MC, DFC) and Charles Steele of 48 Squadron. He had earned a DFC while with 48 and was badly wounded during the raid. He recovered and in the fullness of time retired as Air Marshal Sir Charles Steele KCB, DFC.

Alexander Urinowski had been a fruit broker in Liverpool before the war and his brother was Bill Courtenay, the well known inter-war flier who wrote of his experiences in a book entitled *Airman Friday*. The reason for the difference in surname was that Courtenay had changed his.

Also killed was Lieutenant Alexander Matthews, an American serving with Sholto Douglas' 84 Squadron. Matthews was a friend of Elliott Springs. (See the Wareghem American Cemetery entry in *Airfields and Airmen; Ypres* page 151.There is also an explanation of the American policy on repatriation.) It would seem that his body was repatriated to the United States, as there is no record of him in any of the United States cemeteries in France.

Other ranks receive little attention compared to the officers, particularly those who were pilots and observers. Here are the details of the three airmen killed in the raid on Bertangles:

Airman First Class Leonard Pole 14496 (XVIA C21)

Pole was born on 4 January 1895, in Leicester and before the war had been a motor engineer and driver for British United for four years. He enlisted in the army on 9 September 1914, reaching the rank of corporal. On 21 January 1916, he transferred to the RFC with the rank of acting corporal and on the formation of the RAF on 1 April 1918, he was re-graded as Airman First Class.

Private Patrick Docherty 143021 (XVIA C18)

Before the war Docherty had been a butcher and on 28 November 1914, he enlisted in the Army Service Corps. Serving in France from November 1915 until November 1916, he then spent some time with RFC training units in the UK in his trade as cook. He had joined 85 Squadron before it left for France. In August 1917 and again in January 1918 he had been absent for thirteen and ten days respectively. He left a wife in Paisley, Glasgow.

Airman Second Class Adam Mann 123954 (XVIA C19)

Born in 1899, Mann also hailed from Glasgow. He had enlisted on 23 January 1918, and on 17 May was posted from 91 Squadron to 85 Squadron. In civilian life he was a turner and was only nineteen when he was killed.

All of the other ranks were buried at Amiens Military Hospital at Dury, just south of Amiens, and were later moved to the cemetery at Villers-Bretonneux.

Continue north on the D23 to Corbie. In Corbie follow the D23 and signs to Albert. About one kilometre from Corbie centre join the D1 signposted to Bray-sur-Somme. After about two kilometres a derelict brickworks with a chimney will appear on the left. Park just before reaching the brickworks.

The Morlancourt Ridge

The Ste Colette brickworks, the scene of von Richthofen's fatal crash, must be the most well known non-aerodrome or cemetery aviation site on the Western Front. Every time I have been here there always seems to be someone else visiting the place. In industrialised Britain old buildings are demolished and areas "re-developed". However, it seems that in France buildings remain derelict or empty for years and nobody can be bothered to demolish them. The brickworks here are a case in point. They have been disused for ages and so, consequently, their continued existence gives visitors like ourselves a recognisable feature to relate to. The chimney though is believed not to be the original 1918 one and also is in a slightly different position.

The Ste Colette brickworks looking southwest towards Corbie.

The brickworks looking east.

Manfred von Richthofen

Born on 2 May 1892, in Breslau, von Richthofen was the elder of two brothers. Lothar, younger by two years, was also a successful fighter pilot. He served under his brother in *Jasta* 11 and ultimately commanded it. Lothar too earned the *Pour le Mérite* and, though he survived the war, was killed in a flying accident in 1922.

Manfred began his military career as a cadet in 1909 before joining a Uhlan (or cavalry) regiment as a trainee officer. On the outbreak of war his regiment was sent to the Russian Front. When he came to the Western Front he was awarded the Iron Cross 2nd Class - the first of many decorations the German states were to bestow on him. In May

1915 he transferred to the Air Service and, after qualifying as an observer, he again returned to the Russian Front, with *FA* 69. In the autumn of that year he served with a bomber unit but then undertook pilot training. On graduation he was posted in March 1916 to *KG* 2, a two-seater unit operating on the Verdun front. Despite the fact this was a two-seater unit he was able to fly a single seat Fokker occasionally. Once again von Richthofen found himself back on the Russian Front, when his unit was posted there.

However, in the early autumn of 1916 the first single-seat scouts units or *Jagdstaffeln*, were forming and Oswald Boelcke was recruiting talent for his *Jasta* 2. He had met von Richthofen during a visit he had made to the Eastern Front. Von Richthofen arrived at *Jasta* 2 on 1 September 1916. Boelcke was Germany's most

Manfred von Richthofen, Germany's most successful fighter pilot and the highest scoring ace of the First World War.

successful fighter pilot and a national hero. The acknowledged 'Father of Air Fighting Tactics' and holder of the *Pour le Mérite*, he chose his recruits well and several of them became successful fighter pilots and holders of the coveted Blue Max. Within six weeks he was dead, having collided with one of his new pilots, Erwin Böhme. (See *Airfields and Airmen: Ypres* page 136 for details of Böhme's career.)

Von Richthofen brought down his first machine, an FE2b of 11 Squadron RFC on 17 September 1916. The observer, Captain Tom Rees, was killed and the pilot, Second Lieutenant Lionel Morris, died shortly after of his wounds. (See Porte-de-Paris Cemetery entry in *Airfields and Airmen: Cambrai* Chapter Three.)

On 4 January 1917, he brought down his 16th victim and eight days later was awarded the *Pour le Mérite*. In March he was appointed to the command of a new unit, *Jasta* 11, and promoted to *Oberleutnant*. In the RFC's infamous Bloody April of 1917, when they suffered enormous casualties, von Richthofen claimed twenty-one British machines. In June he was given command of *Jagdgeschwader* 1, comprising *Jasta*s 4, 6, 10 and his own *Jasta* 11. His run of victories came to a sudden temporary halt on 6 July 1917, when he was wounded in the head during a combat with the FE2s of 20 Squadron, though he returned in August.

In March 1918 the Germans launched their Operation Michael using fresh troops released from the Eastern Front by the collapse of Russia. The Germans came perilously close to breaking through and finishing the war before the Americans could effectively enter the conflict. *JG* 1 was in the thick of it and in March and April von Richthofen claimed another seventeen Allied aircraft. However, gone were the easy days of 1917 - now the RFC was equipped with Sopwith Camels, SE5a's, Sopwith Dolphins, Bristol Fighters and, moreover, were deploying them in ever increasing numbers. Battles were becoming more furious and many of Manfred's colleagues had become casualties. A number of friends and senior officers had encouraged him to retire and take up a ground post, where his experience could be put to good use. But he had resisted them and remained at the Front. He was tired and it did not require much mathematical calculation to see that the odds were not on his side. Inevitably, one day his luck would run out.

Last victories

On 20 April 1918, von Richthofen claimed his last two victories in a scrap with No.3 Squadron Royal Air Force. (The RFC and Royal Naval Air Service had combined on 1 April 1918, to form the new service.) Second Lieutenant David Greswolde Lewis of No. 3 Squadron, von Richthofen's last victim, survived his shooting down by the Red Baron and in the May 1934 edition of the magazine *Popular Flying* recounted his experiences of that day:

> *Later I was told I was to be sent to France, and rather than be posted to a squadron the members of which I would not know, I wired to Captain Douglas Bell, whom I knew well, and who had preceded me to the front, to try and get me into No. 3 Squadron, under the command of Major Raymond Barker M.C. In due course I was posted to No. 3, and on arrival at the Squadron, to my great joy, I was placed in Captain Bell's flight.*

> *On the 20th April, a stormy spring day, orders were received for two Flights to carry out an offensive patrol over the enemy lines. We were delayed in our departure by the bad weather, but*

in the evening the weather cleared somewhat, so the twelve small Sopwith Scouts roared into the air and made for the lines. Captain Bell was leading the formation, which included the C.O., and he took us above the clouds where we would be safer from the annoying attentions of the anti-aircraft guns. On arrival above the clouds I was dismayed to find that the other flight of six machines which was to meet us, was not to be seen, nor did they later join us. Captain Bell was not the man to be deterred by the dwindling of his command, so we proceeded, and were soon about four miles in enemy territory and about 9,000 feet from the ground.

Suddenly, in the distance, I saw about fifteen enemy triplanes, and carefully watched Bell so as not to miss any signal he might give. The expected signal was soon to be given and it was - attack!

Almost immediately after this, the enemy, who were flying at right angles to our direction of flight, changed their course, and made to get behind and above us, but Bell frustrated this movement and we met head on, streams of lead spluttering from our guns. Then the "dogfight" started, and worthy opponents we had, for it was part of Richthofen's famous Circus. Bell saved me early in the fight by chasing a "tripe" off my tail.

At this moment I saw one of our machines catch fire, explode, lose a wing and fall earthwards a mass of burning wreckage. I later learned that this was Major Barker. Little did I know that later I was to hurtle earthwards with my machine burning fiercely.

I then saw a bright blue machine slightly below me, and impetuously dived on him. I think I should have stayed above him, and so been more or less on an equality in height with the triplanes, whose lift (because of three planes) was greater than the Camels. I saw my tracer bullets enter this machine but do not think I did him any damage, for I had to turn round to save myself from bullets which I could see were ripping the fabric off my machine. I saw at once that my attacker was Richthofen himself, who had probably been waiting for some indiscreet pilot to get well below him. Then started a merry waltz; round and round, up and down to the staccato of the machine guns of the other fighters. Only once did I get my sights on his machine, but in a trice the positions were reversed, and I felt he was so much my master that he would get me sooner or later. Try as I would

I simply could not shake him off my tail, and all the time the bullets from his hungry Spandaus plastered my machine.

His first burst shattered the compass in front of my face, the liquid there-from "fogging" my goggles, of which, however, I was relieved when a bullet severed the elastic from the frame, and they went over the side. My position was not improved, however, for my eyes filled with water caused by the rush of the wind. Flying and landing wires struck by the bullets folded up before my eyes and struts splintered before that withering fire. I do not think Richthofen was more than 50 feet from me all this time, for I could plainly see his begoggled and helmeted face, and his machine-guns.

Next I heard the sound of flames and the stream of bullets ceased. I turned round to find that my machine was on fire. My petrol tank was alight. I put my machine into a vertical nose dive and raced earthwards in an endeavour to drive the flames upwards and away from me, but every now and then the flames overtook the speed of the machine and were blown back into my face. When about 500 feet from the ground the flames seem to have subsided, so I pulled the control back to gain a horizontal position and was horrified to find that the machine would not answer to the elevators. I held the stick back instinctively, I suppose, and then noticed that the aeroplane was very slowly attaining the desired position, and I thought I should be able to land on an even keel.

This was not to be however. I hit the ground at terrific speed but was hurled from the machine unhurt, except for minor burns and bruises which kept me in Cambrai Hospital for six weeks. I later saw that not a stitch of fabric was left between my seat and the tail, but noticed that a few strips of the material left on my elevators had saved me. The back of my Sidcot suit was in charred strips and my helmet crumpled up when I took it off. I also had one bullet through my trouser leg and one through my sleeve.

Major Barker's machine was burning fiercely not far from me, so I went over to see if I could pull his body out, but was hopelessly beaten by the flames. A German officer assured me that they would decently bury his remains.

Richthofen came down to within 200 feet and waved to me, although I foolishly imagined at first that he was going to make sure of me. I returned his greeting. I was told that I was to see

and talk to him that evening, but did not have the honour of meeting him. I was, of course, a prisoner for the rest of the war.
Lewis was repatriated from prisoner of war camp and returned to his native Southern Rhodesia in December 1918. He died on 10 August 1978, having outlived his victor by more than 60 years.

Another member of that patrol on 20 April 1918, was an American, Curtis Kinney, serving with the RAF. Kinney came from Mount Vernon, Ohio, and after attending the Massachusetts Institute of Technology he had worked in an architectural office in New York. One of the projects he worked on was the Woolworth building. When America entered the war in 1917 he applied to join the US Air Service but was turned down due to defective hearing. Applying to the RFC and lying about his age, as he was nearly 29 years old, he was accepted. After training in Canada he sailed for the UK and was posted to No. 3 Squadron at Warloy, where he arrived in early March 1918. In his autobiography *I Flew a Camel* he described the patrol:

On April 20 the weather was mostly dud and there was little flying so I read and wrote letters. At four o'clock I went to tea at the mess as usual, where I had a steaming hot cup and helped myself to sardines - a rare treat. At five o'clock an officer entered hurriedly and went to the front table, where he called for our attention in a flat voice. We were told that A and C Flights were to prepare for flight at once. Lorne and I got up and went to our quarters for our flying gear, then made for the field and got into our machines. The engines were warmed and ready. Eleven of us took off on an offensive patrol of two flights, each flight in V formation. I had no idea where we were headed but this was not unusual. The briefing generally ended with the flight commanders; we merely followed. What was unusual about this patrol, however, was that our C.O., Maj. R. Raymond-Barker, accompanied us. As the chief administration officer he rarely flew although he had gained seven victories and earned the Military Cross. C Flight led the patrol, Major Raymond-Barker in the forefront with Capt. "Ginger" Bell, Lt. Jack Riley, Lt. Lloyd Hamilton; an American from Burlington, Vermont, Lieutenant Squires, and Lt. D. G. "Babe" Lewis, a Rhodesian colonial who had only recently completed his pre-combat flying and was now on his first offensive patrol. Lewis had been given the nickname "Babe" because he was only eighteen, the youngest pilot in the squadron. In A Flight were Captain Leman, an Englishman; three Canadians, Lts. Bill Boyd, Victor McElroy,

Lorne McIntyre; and myself, an American.

Our two flights lost contact because we took off at different intervals and because of the still squally weather. The entire front was overhung with low, dark clouds. But Captain Leman, undisturbed by the separation, kept a straight course. We eventually found C Flight after about an hour, scrambled up in a widespread dogfight and outnumbered by a large group of brightly coloured Fokker triplanes. As we approached, directly in front of me, a Camel turned on its side and plummeted to the earth leaving a trail of thick black smoke. I couldn't take my eyes from the terrible sight. What a ghastly way to die, burned to death in the sky! If any pain-wracked life remained during the plunge it ended on violent impact with the earth. I only had time to think: "... the poor devil...not a chance in the world..." then I was in the midst of it. I suddenly saw the flash of a bright red triplane looming before me - the most terrifying thing I had seen in the air. I wanted to turn west and scram! But something wouldn't let me. Instead, I pointed my nose at the red devil and pressed my Vickers gun controls. Both machine guns opened up and I saw my tracers going towards the fuselage of the red fighter. At the same time I heard a distinct pop-pop-pop right behind me and thin blue threads of tracer bullets passed through my wing planes, much too close for comfort. I risked a quick glance backwards and saw a green and white triplane bearing down on me. To save myself from becoming another fiery furnace like the one I had just seen I jammed on right rudder and pushed the control stick forward and right to make myself an impossible target. My Camel responded beautifully by immediately snapping into a spin with full engine on. I held her there for a few seconds and then straightened out. When I looked around there wasn't a plane to be seen in the sky. Like most dogfights it was a quick encounter, in for the kill and out.

The death of a legend

The day following the Raymond-Barker and Lewis battle began slightly drizzly, but this gave way to mist and haze later in the morning. Von Richthofen's aerodrome at Cappy was shrouded in fog but at 1030 the machines of *Jasta* 11 took off to pursue British aircraft reported on their front. At almost the same time, three sections of five machines each from 209 Squadron were lifting off at Bertangles for a High Offensive Patrol.

145

The Camels of B Flight, led by an American, Oliver Le Boutillier, found and shot down an Albatros two-seater south of the Amiens to St Quentin road. On their way north they encountered von Richthofen and his men about to engage RE8s of No. 3 Squadron Australian Flying Corps. No. 3 AFC were to play a significant role in the von Richthofen episode. The *Jasta* 11 Triplanes, supported by Albatros DVs of *Jasta* 5, began to scrap with the 209 Squadron Camels over the Somme valley. During the fight Wilfred 'Wop' May, a Canadian from Edmonton, Alberta kept to the edge of the fray where, as a new pilot, he had been advised to stay. A Fokker passed near him and he was tempted to have a crack at it but was in turn attacked from behind by another Triplane. May broke away for the safety of the Allied lines pursued by the Fokker. The pursuit continued at very low level along the winding Somme valley with May desperately trying to shake off the red machine. Coming to a bend to the left taking him back into German held territory May had no alternative but to turn right, haul back on the stick and zoom up and over the top of the Morlancourt Ridge. Roy Brown, May's flight commander and an experienced pilot, had seen his predicament and dived out of the dogfight to go to his assistance. He pursued and fired at the red Triplane. As they passed over the Allied front line on top of the ridge, the red triplane wobbled and then went down and crashed near the Ste Colette brickworks. The machine made a clumsy landing, wiping off the undercarriage but remaining upright. Von Richthofen was found dead in the cockpit, killed by a single shot through the chest.

What made von Richthofen pursue May at such low level, thereby breaking his own basic rules? He must have known he would be under heavy ground fire as he approached the enemy front line on top of the Morlancourt Ridge. Unusually, there was strong wind from the east that day, which may have blown him over the Allied lines much quicker than he anticipated, or perhaps he was just too intent on scoring his 81st victory.

The red Fokker and von Richthofen's body were retrieved by a party

Sopwith Camels of 209 Squadron in late 1918. The squadron marking of three bars had been introduced shortly before the von Richthofen action.

Captain Roy Brown DSC, commanding A Flight of 209 Squadron.

from No. 3 Squadron Australian Flying Corps and removed to their aerodrome at Bertangles. From what had been a virtually complete Fokker Triplane when it landed, souvenir hunters had reduced the machine to an unrecognisable pile of pieces. Von Richthofen had collected serial numbers, engine parts and other items from his victims and adorned his room at home with them. Ironically he had now become the great 'souvenired'. The pieces of his machine are now scattered around the world with the largest part, the engine, residing in the Imperial War Museum in London.

The aftermath

From almost the moment he died von Richthofen's loss has been surrounded by controversy. The RAF understandably decided that Roy Brown in his Camel of 209 Squadron was the victor and in fact the official squadron crest today reflects this, for it depicts an eagle falling. The Australians, who were occupying the Morlancourt Ridge also, naturally, believed that one of their machine gunners fired the fatal shot. There have been countless books written about the Red Baron and he continues to hold as big a fascination today as he has ever done.

The official squadron crest of 209 Squadron. Motto: Might and Main. The falling eagle symbolises their part in the shooting down of von Richthofen on 21 April 1918.

Many books have been written about him and not a year passes without yet another one being published and raking over the same old ground. Of the many books on the subject, the best are listed in the bibliography at the end of this guide.

The most scientific, detailed and reasoned volume concerning the events and various claims of 21 April 1918 is *The Red Baron's Last Flight* by Norman Franks and Alan Bennett. It examines pathological and ballistic analyses, together with a re-examination of the original autopsies and eyewitness accounts. I have my opinion on the events of that day but leave it to the reader to make his or her own judgement.

Continue on the D1 for approximately four kilometres and then turn left on the D42 to Morlancourt and Albert. This concludes the southern area tour.

The Eastern Area

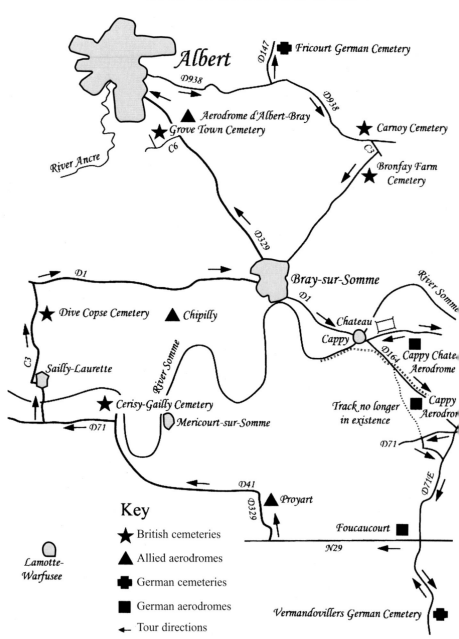

Albert

D147 — Fricourt German Cemetery

D938

D938

▲ Aerodrome d'Albert-Bray

★ Grove Town Cemetery

★ Carnoy Cemetery

C6

C3

River Ancre

★ Bronfay Farm Cemetery

D329

Bray-sur-Somme

River Somme

D1

D1

▲ Chipilly

★ Dive Copse Cemetery

Chateau

Cappy

D164

■ Cappy Chate Aerodrome

C3

River Somme

Sailly-Laurette

Track no longer in existence

■ Cappy Aerodro

★ Cerisy-Gailly Cemetery

Méricourt-sur-Somme

D71

D71

D71E

D41

D329

▲ Proyart

Key

★ British cemeteries

▲ Allied aerodromes

✚ German cemeteries

■ German aerodromes

← Tour directions

Lamotte-Warfusee

Foucaucourt ■

N29

Vermandovillers German Cemetery ✚

148

Chapter Three

SOMME: THE EASTERN AREA

Most of this tour is in the area predominantly occupied by the Germans. It was abandoned by them when they retreated to the Hindenburg Line in early 1917 but retaken in March 1918. The Allies re-captured it in August 1918 during the offensive which brought the war to an end. The sites that will be visited on this tour, together with the principal points of interest are:

Fricourt German Cemetery - Braun and the giant aeroplanes of *Rfa* 501
Carnoy Military Cemetery - Major Balcombe-Brown, of 56 Squadron
Bronfay Farm British Military Cemetery - Sergeant W J Middleton DFM
Cappy Aerodrome - *Jagdgeschwader* 1 and von Richthofen's last flight
Vermandovillers German Cemetery - Hans Weiss, *Jasta* 11
Foucaucourt Aerodrome - Rudolph Stark and *Jastas* 34 and 77b
Cerisy-Gailly Military Cemetery - J J Petre, Co of No. 6(N)
Dive Copse Military Cemetery - G H Harding 79 Squadron
Grove Town Military Cemetery - a collision with a kite balloon

Leave Albert on the D938, the Peronne road. After about four kilometres turn left on the D147 to Fricourt. Proceed through the village and the German cemetery is just north on the right side of the road.

Fricourt German Cemetery

There are few German cemeteries in the Somme area and they contain only a fraction of the German casualties. This is the only one located in the 1916 British Battle of the Somme area and in terms of burials is the second largest in the Somme *département* after Vermandovillers. There are four equal sections numbered from left to right as you enter and at the back is a *Kameradengrab*. The names of the known are commemorated on 42 bronze plaques and are listed in alphabetical order from left to right. The total number of burials in the cemetery is 17,027.

It was here that Manfred von Richthofen's body was brought after the war from the village cemetery at Bertangles before being disinterred again in 1925 and taken to Berlin.

There are a number of fliers here and most of them are named on the *Kameradengrab* panels. The first of three we have come to see is Johannes Braun.

Johannes Braun and the giant R-Plane

Braun was born on 2 September 1881, in Cologne and in 1918 was flying with *Rfa* 501. This unit operated giant Staaken aeroplanes on bombing attacks against Allied installations. On the night of 10/11 August 1918 he and his crew failed to return from one such operation. He was a *Leutnant* and as the only observer, with the other two officers being pilots, it is probable he was the commander of the aeroplane. In the German Air Service the observer commanded the aeroplane and the pilot could be of quite a low rank.

In the summer of 1913 one of the many aviation prizes established by the Daily Mail was one for the first pilot to cross the Atlantic in an aeroplane. The sum involved was £10,000 - a fortune in those days. Several companies initiated designs but the outbreak of war put an end to most of these proposals. One project in Germany, however, continued when Count von Zeppelin and the firm of Hirth-Klein combined to design a machine capable of carrying a large bomb load over a great distance. In September 1914 construction of the first of a relatively small number of these Staaken giant bombers was started. German military aeroplanes were categorised by a prefix letter. C was the designation for single-engined armed biplanes; D for single-seat, single engined armed biplanes; G for armed biplanes with more than

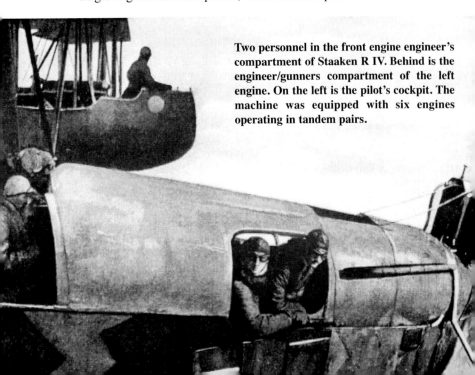

Two personnel in the front engine engineer's compartment of Staaken R IV. Behind is the engineer/gunners compartment of the left engine. On the left is the pilot's cockpit. The machine was equipped with six engines operating in tandem pairs.

one engine; and R for armed biplanes with three to six engines. The letter R was an abbreviation for *Riesenflugzeug* or giant aircraft. The Staaken was not the only type in this category, as several other companies manufactured their own designs.

The specification for this type of machine was very detailed. There was a requirement for multiple engines and the unique ability to service or repair these in flight, in order to confer greater reliability. A number of variants were built with either four or five engines.

Two squadrons, *Riesenfluzeugabteilungen* (or *Rfa*) were formed to operate these giant machines and received the designations *Rfa* 500 and 501. The R planes were initially deployed against the Russians on the Eastern Front but were then transferred to the west where, together with Gotha bombers, they were engaged on night bombing of London. In May 1918 the Staakens were switched from the bombing of London to military targets in France. The R planes were designed for long-range bombing; short-range operations were inefficient due to the amount of time it required to arm and refuel them. The smaller Gothas could be serviced more quickly and were able to carry out more than one operation in a night. During this phase the Giants suffered their only casualties to enemy action, with one being brought down by French anti-aircraft fire and two by fighters from No. 151 Squadron RAF.

The Staaken type of machine was huge and an extremely intimidating opponent. With a wingspan of 138 feet, it was very nearly twice the size of the large Gotha bomber. German night attacks on the Allied rear areas had become such a problem by 1918 that a specialist night fighter unit was formed. No. 151 Squadron arrived in France on 23 June 1918, equipped with Sopwith Camels modified for flying at night. They had the unique distinction of being the first offensive night

Staaken R43, the machine shot down by Yuille. The size of the machine can be gauged by the two small figures to the left of the right hand engine.

Captain A B Yuille DFC, 151 Squadron.

fighter unit. The Home Defence squadrons in the UK were purely defensive but 151 was charged with both defending and also taking the war to the enemy over their aerodromes.

Archibald Buchanan Yuille was born on 6 November 1896, in Calcutta, but came from Northwood in Middlesex. After service in the 3rd Battalion of the East Lancashire Regiment, where he reached the rank of Captain, he joined the RFC in the autumn of 1917. Some months were spent with 112 Squadron, a Home Defence unit, and then he became part of 151 when it formed. Owing to periods in hospital he spent only three months on operations, but in that time brought down two German machines at night.

On the night of 10/11 August 1918, Yuille was patrolling just south of Doullens at 8,000 feet. Patrol heights at night were considerably lower than for daytime. The necessity for the bombers to maintain altitude to avoid enemy fighters was more than compensated for by their invisibility in the darkness. Searching for an enemy machine at night without radar was literally like searching for a needle in a haystack. Fortunately, anti-aircraft ground defences were able to illuminate attacking bombers for the marauding Camels of 151 Squadron. Yuille was attracted by some searchlights probing for a target and closing on the beams he found an enemy machine. Even though another of his colleagues was firing on it, he closed to only twenty yards and shot it down. With a target of this size it was very easy to open fire from long range, believing you were much closer. The Staaken's armament was formidable with six machine guns, including two that were in upper wing nacelles and one that fired below the fuselage through a tunnel.

Five of the crew attempted to parachute to safety but all nine crewmembers were killed. The Staaken was of great interest to British Intelligence and despite the wreckage seemingly only consisting of fragments, the RAF technical team were able to glean an extraordinary

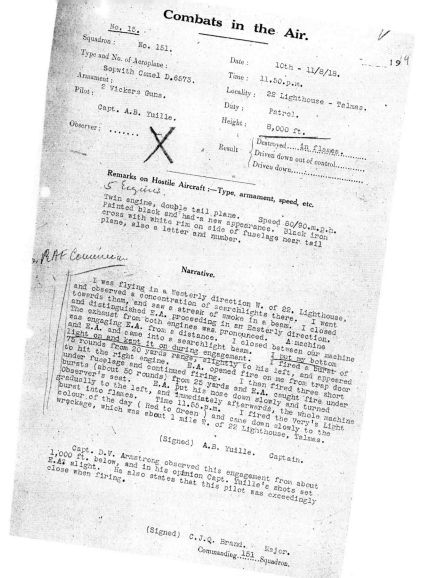

Combats in the Air.

No. 15.

19 4

Squadron : No. 151.

Type and No. of Aeroplane :
Sopwith Camel D.6573.

Armament : 2 Vickers Guns.

Pilot : Capt. A.B. Yuille.

Observer : ....

Date : 10th - 11/8/18.

Time : 11.50.p.m.

Locality : 22 Lighthouse - Talmas.

Duty : Patrol.

Height : 8,000 ft.

Result { Destroyed.....in flames.......
{ Driven down out of control..........
{ Driven down.....................

X

Remarks on Hostile Aircraft :—Type, armament, speed, etc.

5 Engines

Twin engine, double tail plane.
Painted black and had a new appearance.   Speed 80/90.m.p.h.
cross with white rim on side of fuselage   Black iron
plane, also a letter and number.   near tail

RAF Commission

Narrative.

I was flying in a Westerly direction W. of 22. Lighthouse,
and observed a concentration of searchlights there.   I went
towards them, and saw a streak of smoke in a beam. I closed
and distinguished E.A. Proceeding in an Easterly direction.
The exhaust from both engines was pronounced. A machine
was engaging E.A. from a distance. I closed between our machine
and E.A. and came into a searchlight beam. I put my bottom
light on and kept it on during engagement. I fired a burst of
75 rounds from 20 yards range, slightly to his left, and appeared
to hit the right engine. E.A. opened fire on me from trap door
under fuselage and continued firing. I then fired three short
bursts (about 50 rounds) from 25 yards and E.A. caught fire under
Observer's seat. E.A. put his nose down slowly and turned
gradually to the left, and immediately afterwards, the whole machine
burst into flames. Time 11.55.p.m.   I fired the Very's Light
colour of the day (Red to Green) and came down slowly to the
wreckage, which was about 1 mile W. of 22 Lighthouse, Talmas.

(Signed) A.B. Yuille.   Captain.

Capt. D.V. Armstrong observed this engagement from about
1,000 ft. below, and in his opinion Capt. Yuille's shots set
E.A. alight. He also states that this pilot was exceedingly
close when firing.

(Signed) C.J.Q. Brand. Major.
Commanding......151.....Squadron.

The combat report filed by Yuille after his action on the night of 10/11 August 1918.

amount of information. Surprisingly, it was found that two of the weapons on board were captured British Lewis machine guns. The machine was allocated the number G/ 3 Brigade/10 and was the subject of a detailed report. (The designation indicated that this was the tenth German machine to fall in 3 Brigade's area.)

In November 1918 the citation for Yuille's DFC was announced:

The wreckage of Staaken R 43 at Talmas, south of Vert Galand.

One night during the recent operations when on patrol this officer observed an enemy aeroplane in the beams of a searchlight. Three of our 'Camels' were engaging this machine, but not at sufficiently close range for decisive results. With great gallantry he dived between the nearest 'Camel' and the enemy, thereby exposing himself to the fire of our tracers, and by skilful manoeuvre succeeded in getting under the tail of the enemy machine, where he opened fire at twenty-five yards. After three bursts the enemy machine caught fire and crashed. A fine performance, deserving the highest praise.

Of the nine crew members only Johannes Braun appears to be buried in France. It is impossible to say whether the other eight were unidentifiable or if their remains were returned to Germany after the war.

The scattered remains of Staaken R 43. The combat and crash were seen by personnel on the aerodrome at Vert Galand.

Oberleutnant Walter Ewers - CO of *Jasta* 77b

Also in the mass grave are two other interesting individuals. The German air service suffered as many losses of commanding officers as did their opponents in the RFC and RNAS. It is probably true to say, though, that German commanding officers were expected to lead their men in the air, whereas the RFC had at one stage a policy of forbidding theirs from flying, in order to preserve experience.

Walter Ewers was born in Lubeck on 11 May 1892, and had served in the Bavarian Field Artillery Regiment Nr.7 before joining the air service in 1917. He claimed three Allied machines while flying with *Jasta* 12 and then on 21 January 1918, was posted to *Jagdstaffel* 77b. This unit, as the suffix denotes, was a Bavarian unit and had been formed on 25 November 1917, under the command of *Oberleutnant* Otto Diendl, who had previously served in *Jasta* 1. Ewers claimed the unit's first three victories and then when Diendl was posted to a flying school he took command. Initially fighting against the French, *Jasta* 77b was transferred to 2 *Armee* front on 27 March 1918 and a month later they moved to Foucaucourt aerodrome. (See the Foucaucourt entry later in the chapter.)

In addition to the Iron Cross First Class, Ewers also received the Bavarian Military Merit Order Fourth Class with Swords and the Knight's Cross of the Hohenzollern House Order.

At 0930 hours on 15 May 1918, he was shot down and killed during a battle over Villers-Bretonneux. It is believed he was brought down by a Sopwith Camel from 65 Squadron.

Oberleutnant **Walter Ewers, commanding Bavarian *Jasta* 77b.**

Rudolph Stark, who was serving in *Jasta* 34b and was appointed temporary commander of *Jasta* 77b, recounted Ewer's funeral and his feelings of the war in his autobiography *Wings of War*:

The leader of Jagdstaffel 77 fell in an air fight. His body will be sent home.

A tent-hangar stands open wide; its vast interior shows black against the sky. In this tent lies the coffin. Two machines stand as silent sentinels about the catafalque.

Young May greenery rustles in the gentle breeze.

A priest speaks solemn words.

155

Ewer's funeral on Foucaucourt aerodrome.

Funeral music resounds over the aerodrome.

The coffin is born on the shoulders of comrades from the Staffel. Slowly the procession begins to move. For the last time the leader crosses his aerodrome. Round the car his comrades say their last farewell to the dead; then he starts his long journey homeward.

We stand there with bowed heads and clenched hands. We have little to say to one another, for we know that our destiny is the same. It may come soon, it may come later.

The spring heaven laughs in radiant blue. From near and far we hear the songs of propellers. Shrapnel clouds line the horizon. The war goes on and drags us out to combat.

Leutnant Heinrich Georg Geigl - CO of *Jasta* 16b

Geigl was yet another Bavarian *Jasta* commander to fall in action.

Leutnant Heinrich Georg Geigl *Jasta* 16b

He came from Bad Abbach in Bavaria and was 23 years old when the war commenced. Before joining up he had been a philosophy student and a teacher. After service in *Kaghol* 6 he had transferred to Bavarian *Jasta* 34. They were based on the French sector of the lines and during his service with this unit he claimed five French machines. On 17 August 1917, he was given command of another Bavarian *Jagdstaffel*, number 16, still located on the French front. After only three days in command he was wounded by ground fire, while flying low over French trenches but on recovery continued in command. In the first week of February 1918 *Jasta* 16 were transferred to the Flanders front as part of 4 *Armee*, and then in mid-March were further moved down to the Somme with 2 *Armee*.

156

Albatros DIII D2114/16 of *Jasta* 16b. Note the highly varnished plywood fuselage.

They were stationed at Foucaucourt from 21 March until 6 April 1918. Two days before the move they were involved in a combat with Camels over Warfusee and it is believed Geigl collided with Camel D6552 of 65 Squadron, flown by Second Lieutenant J G Kennedy. Kennedy was credited to Geigl as his thirteenth and final victim. James Gilbert Kennedy was at first thought to be captive in the prisoner of war camp at Clausthal but this report was erroneous. In fact he had been killed and his body was never found.

Return to the D938 through the centre of Fricourt. Turn left along the D938 towards Peronne. After approximately two kilometres turn left at the second sign to Carnoy, just after the green Commonwealth War Graves Commission sign. The cemetery is a short distance down the road on the left.

Carnoy Military Cemetery

The cemetery (10/94) was begun in August 1915 and was used until July 1916, when the Battle of the Somme began. As the British lines moved forward, the Field Ambulances followed the advance. It was closed in March 1917 but from March until August 1918 was used by the Germans. A separate German cemetery was also established alongside. In 1924 the German graves, plus the adjacent German cemetery were removed, leaving 850 Allied casualties. After the war Carnoy was adopted by the city of Swansea.

The first time I ever visited this spot it was a lovely warm summer's day and the insects were buzzing and there was not another noise to be heard. Perfect tranquillity, and a complete contrast to what the scene must have been like in the Great War.

At the rear of the cemetery against the wall are some special memorials. Two of these are to Lieutenant E H Piper and Second Lieutenant H L B Crabbe of 57 Squadron, who were killed on 15 May 1918, in the same patrol as Mond and Martyn, whose memorial entry is in the previous chapter.

To the left side of the cemetery near the front, on the end of a row is the grave (G50) of Major Rainsford Balcombe-Brown, commanding officer of 56 Squadron.

56 Squadron and the SE5

Number 56 Squadron was officially formed on 6 April 1916, at Gosport near Portsmouth. Command of the unit passed through several hands, including that of H D Harvey-Kelly until the arrival on 6 February 1917, of Major R G Blomfield. He was destined to take the squadron to France. Cecil Lewis wrote in his autobiography *Sagittarius Rising*:

> *The success of a squadron depends enormously on the personality of the Commanding Officer. Major Bloomfield (sic), O.C. 56, was determined to allow nothing to come between him and making his the crack fighting squadron in the R.F.C. His geniality did not prevent him being very sharp-eyed and nimble-witted. Efficiency was his watchword.*
>
> *Tremendously energetic and keen, he was always to be seen hurrying here and there, giving close personal supervision to every detail of the squadron's work - activity and organisation*

The 56 Squadron orchestra. Seated in the centre with a violin is the leader, Sergeant P E Gayer.

*personified. He had all his pilots out for a run before breakfast,
kept them busy round the sheds all day, and turned them loose in
town at night. They had to be tip-top aviators and bring down
Huns. Nothing else mattered.*

He was very successful at this, and his first great coup was to have
Albert Ball posted to his squadron. Ball was at this time Britain's most
successful fighter pilot and a national hero. Not only this but Ball in
turn recruited or headhunted the best for 56 Squadron, including
friends from his 60 Squadron days. All three flight commanders were
very experienced and capable fighter pilots. In addition Blomfield
arranged to have the best mechanics posted to his command and,
believing music was a great morale booster, had those tradesmen who
were also musicians sent to 56. The squadron orchestra was the envy
of the RFC. When the officers were invited to other squadrons they
were asked to bring their orchestra with them.

Lastly, and possibly the most important factor in the squadron's
favour, was that they would be the first unit to take the new Royal
Aircraft Factory SE5 to France. Since the bloodbath of 'Bloody April',
when the RFC struggled through with obsolescent machines, they were
now equipping with better aeroplanes that would turn the tide.

On 7 April 1917, thirteen machines crossed the Channel to war and
flew into Vert Galand. Here they joined the Sopwith Pups of 66
Squadron and the Spads of 19 Squadron, commanded by the
redoubtable Harvey-Kelly. The three squadrons made up 9
Headquarters Wing. During the summer of 1917 the squadron
'scoreboard' steadily increased, despite the loss of Ball and other
experienced personnel. In August Blomfield arranged for Jimmy
McCudden to be posted to 56 as a flight commander. McCudden was
to claim some 50 enemy machines during his time with the unit, adding
further lustre to the squadron.

In October Blomfield was posted back home and his replacement
was Richard Balcombe-Brown. Blomfield served in the RAF during
the Second World War but died in 1940 at an early age.

Major Rainsford Balcombe-Brown (G50)

The latter arrived three days early in order to learn the ropes and be
briefed by his predecessor. Blomfield was a difficult act to follow but
to his credit Balcombe-Brown was soon able to gain the respect of the
squadron.

Balcombe-Brown was a New Zealander from Upper Hutt, near
Wellington in North Island. Commissioned into the Royal Field

Major R Balcombe-Brown (left) and Major R G Blomfield, in front of the 56 Squadron commander's office. Note the notice on the door which says 'Enter without Knocking'.

Artillery he joined the RFC, after having gained his 'ticket', in May 1915. From training he went to 1 Squadron RFC at Bailleul on 21 June 1916, and was posted back to Home Establishment in November 1916, having earned an MC. After serving in several training units, Balcombe-Brown returned to France to command 56 Squadron.

At the end of April 1918 Captain E D 'Spider' Atkinson was attached to 56 from the School of Aerial Fighting at Ayr for a refresher course, prior to taking command of a flight in 64 Squadron. Balcombe-Browne and Atkinson had joined 1 Squadron at virtually the same time and had served together for nearly six months. Whether the posting of Atkinson had been 'arranged' is impossible to say, but probably very likely.

Both of them followed a formation of nine 56 Squadron SE5a's on the morning of 2 May 1918 - Atkinson ostensibly to 'see the lines' and Balcombe-Browne on a Special Mission. The latter description, as previously mentioned, was a euphemism that many squadron commanders, who were not allowed to cross the lines, employed to do just that. In a fight over the Somme battlefield the patrol engaged a number of Pfalz DIIIs and Fokker triplanes. Balcombe-Brown was last seen at 1130 hours engaging an enemy machine over Martinpuich, northeast of Albert. On their return to the aerodrome at Valheureux, the patrol put claims in for four enemy machines but Balcombe-Brown failed to return. It would seem he fell foul of *Oberleutnant* Erich Löwenhardt, commanding officer of *Jagdstaffel* 10 and one of Germany's most successful fighter pilots of the Great War.

Balcombe-Brown has the dubious distinction of being the only commanding officer of 56 Squadron to have been killed in the war.

Return to the main road and cross over it on the C3, signposted to Susanne. After a few hundred metres turn right at an unsignposted crossroads. Bronfay Cemetery is on the left in approximately one kilometre.

Bronfay Farm Military Cemetery

The farm on the other side of the road has a large mural of a kite balloon scene on the wall of a barn. Several balloons are depicted flying over the Somme battlefield and the largest one has an unlikely black and white chequered paint scheme.

The cemetery (9/106) is on the side of the road and the graves are in parallel lines to it. The graves of particular interest are in the back row in the far right corner from the entrance, adjacent to the Cross of Sacrifice (II G16, G19 and G21).

It was begun in October 1914 but from August 1915 until February 1917 was used by Allied troops, particularly during the Battle of the Somme. XIV Corps Main Dressing Station was at the adjacent farm. There were more burials here as the battle flowed back and forth across the area during the advances and retreats of 1918. There are now 537 casualties buried here.

The Distinguished Flying Medal

The Royal Air Force was formed on 1 April 1918, and though it was some time before the last vestiges of the RFC and RNAS disappeared, different gallantry awards were soon instituted for the new service. Four new medals were approved, with the Distinguished Flying Cross and Air Force Cross being awarded to officers and warrant officers and the Distinguished Flying Medal and Air Force Medal to NCOs and other ranks. King George V gave his consent for the new awards and this appeared in the London Gazette of 3 June 1918, together with the announcements of the first awards. It was not until 17 December that the King approved in writing the warrants covering the awards. Initially the stripes on the ribbon were horizontal but in July 1919 they were changed to diagonal ones at 45 degrees, running left to right as they remain to this day.

In the last chapter concerning the 1915 Villers-Bretonneux aerodrome and Flight Sergeant J M Hargreaves section, the rarity of the award of the Distinguished Conduct Medal to the flying services was discussed. The DFM was just as rare a decoration, in that during the First World War only 102 were awarded, plus one Bar. (67162 Sergeant Observer Arthur Newland.) The first two were gazetted on 3 June 1918, and a second batch on 21 September 1918.

Sergeant William James Middleton 205 Squadron (II G16)

William James Middleton's DFM appeared in the second group

DH9a E9716 'Y' of 205 Squadron. This machine was delivered shortly before the Armistice and served until January 1919.

gazetted and he has the unique distinction of being the only Great War DFM recipient buried on the Western Front. Though his Commonwealth War Graves Commission entry states he was No.216604 Serjeant RAF, his citation betrays his origins. Number 205 Squadron had been 5 (Naval) Squadron before the formation of the RAF and he had been No. F16604, A.C.1 Gunlayer W J Middleton - a Royal Navy rank.

Middleton was born on 7 May 1897, in Farmingham, Kent, though at the time of his enlistment his parents were living in Woodford Green, Essex. Before joining the Royal Naval Air Service in June 1916 he had been a cordite packer and in his spare time had been assistant scoutmaster with the 2nd Epping Forest Troop of the Boy Scouts. After service at Kingsnorth and Eastchurch he arrived at Dunkirk shortly before Christmas 1917 and was probably posted to 205 Squadron on 1 April 1918. After the formation of the RAF his rank was changed to Sergeant. In May 1918 he received his observer's badge.

His citation read:

> *He has taken part in 67 raids and has shown conspicuous gallantry and skill in bombing enemy lines of communications, dumps and aerodromes. On one occasion he obtained six direct hits in spite of intense anti-aircraft fire.*

Middleton and his pilot, Lieutenant Furze, took off in their DH9a at 0845 on 3 October 1918, from the aerodrome at Proyart East, just south of Bray-sur-Somme, for a low level reconnaissance. They returned at 1020 with Middleton wounded by ground-fire. He died the following day from his wounds.

As well as his DFM, Middleton had also been awarded the French *Médaille d'Honneur*.

One other DFM holder died as a result of enemy action. Sergeant W

G Dyke, a gunner in 18 Squadron RAF, succumbed after arriving in England as a result of wounds. He is buried at Nuneaton, Warwickshire. Dyke is unique, as he was the only person to receive the DCM and DFM in the First World War. Fortunately, his medal group was generously donated to the RAF Museum in recent years by an American, Neal O'Connor, and is on display in the museum at the time of writing. In recent years the DFM has been abolished.

Major A H O'Hara Wood (II G19)

Losses are hard at the best of times and by early October 1918 it must have been obvious that the war was not going to last much longer. For 46 Squadron the last five weeks were particularly sad, as of the six pilots killed, four were lost in mid-air collisions, including their commanding officer, Major O'Hara-Wood. Most poignant of all, the last two casualties occurred only the day before the Armistice.

Arthur Holroyd O'Hara-Wood had been born in Melbourne on 10 January 1890, and had learned to fly at Brooklands, qualifying on 7 November 1915, in a Maurice Farman. After advanced instruction with 20 Squadron and the Central Flying School, he received his first operational posting when sent to No. 10 Squadron at Chocques, north west of Bethune, in February 1916. Flying the BE2c, he was promoted to flight commander five months later and then returned to England a week before Christmas 1916, having completed ten months at the Front. Training appointments in the United Kingdom were followed by a further two-month period in France before being made commanding officer of 46 Squadron on 21 July 1918.

Major A H O'Hara-Wood, commanding 46 Squadron, killed on 4 October 1918.

At 1050 in the morning of 4 October fifteen Sopwith Camels from 46 Squadron lifted off from von Richthofen's old aerodrome at Cappy for an Offensive Patrol in the St Quentin area. Over St Quentin, Captain J Leith, one of the flight commanders, who was flying on O'Hara-Wood's left, saw him do a sudden very sharp 180 degree left turn. Leith followed him round and then saw that his commanding officer was heading straight for Lieutenant L L Saunders coming the other way. Without radio there was no way to shout a warning and in horror he watched the inevitable crash. Neither pilot saw the other, and they met head on, with their right wings smashing into each other. Leith saw O'Hara-Wood's right wings come off and then had himself to do a sharp left turn to avoid the falling wreckage. The machines fell 14,000 feet and there was no hope of survival. Both officers were admitted to 37 Casualty Clearing Station but were dead on arrival. Later in the day Captain D R MacLaren, 46 Squadron's most successful pilot of the First World War with 54 victories, flew a search for the crash site.

Lorne Lamont Saunders, a Canadian from Ontario, had joined 46 Squadron at the end of July 1918. He had spent three weeks in hospital as a result of crashing a Camel while serving with 70 Squadron. He was not to survive his second crash and now lies near his late commanding officer in grave II G21. The end of the war was just five weeks away.

Continue on the road towards Bray-sur-Somme. Turn left on the D329 into the town centre. Just past the church turn left on the D1 to Cappy. The road crosses a wide lagoon and then the canalised river before swinging left up the hill to the chateau.

Cappy Aerodrome

This aerodrome was one of a number of new sites that were established by German air service units as they continued to keep up with the advancing German army in the spring offensive of 1918. Cappy was in fact several aerodromes and the RAF identified two as Cappy and Cappy Chateau. Several units, including two-seater reconnaissance ones, were based here. It is difficult to establish where various *Staffeln* were located and it is possible that *Jasta* 5 were based on the Chateau Aerodrome. The inhabitants of the chateau believe that von Richthofen lived here and this may be true. However, it is also believed that he slept on the aerodrome in a hut.

Return to the centre of Cappy and then turn left on the D164 signposted to Dompierre. On the plateau the road is crossed by a light railway. Stop at this point.

The area to the right of the road is believed to be the aerodrome that was occupied by *Jagdgeschwader* 1 in April and May of 1918. Certainly an RAF reconnaissance photograph of 2 May shows a large concentration of canvas hangars suitable for a formation of four *Jastas*. If so, then it was from here that von Richthofen, the most successful fighter pilot of the Great War, took off on his last flight.

The Cappy Aerodromes

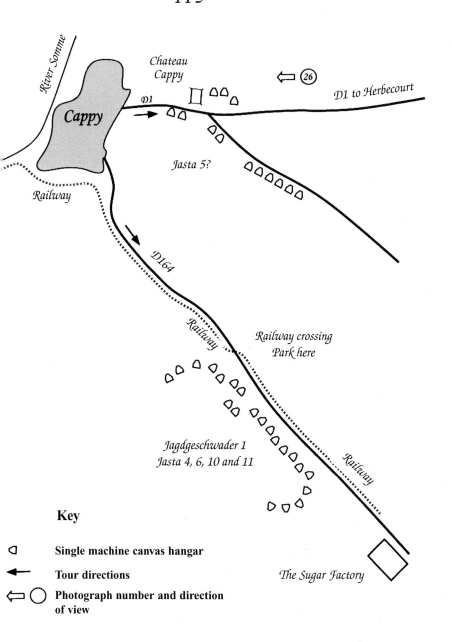

Key

◁   **Single machine canvas hangar**

←   **Tour directions**

⇐ ◯   **Photograph number and direction of view**

Albatros scouts of *Jasta* 5 at Cappy, possibly at the Chateau Aerodrome. On the left is the machine of Paul Baümer (43 victories) and in the centre that of Fritz Rumey (45 victories). Both were awarded the *Pour le Mérite*.

Picture No. 26. The chateau at Cappy looking west, with the village and River Somme in the background.

CHATEAU CAPPY

CHATEAU AERODROME

Von Richthofen's last flight on 21 April 1918

On 21 March 1918, the German army launched its last-ditch attempt to break through the Allied line. In the previous week *Jagdgeschwader* 1 had been busy preparing a new aerodrome at Awoingt, three kilometres south east of Cambrai. The work was done during the night, so that by dawn everything was concealed from the eyes of the prying enemy.

The German offensive crashed through the Allied front line, assisted by fog and mist. Flying was severely curtailed, preventing the RFC and RNAS from supporting the hard pressed infantry. Thick mist also hampered flying on the following day. With the advance of the German forces, *JG* 1 moved forward in support on 26 March to the abandoned British aerodrome at Lechelle, ten kilometres southeast of Bapaume. The RFC had left in such a hurry that the huts and Bessonneau hangars had not been destroyed and were gratefully received by the Germans.

By 8 April the German advance slowed down but, nevertheless, *Jagdgeschwader* 1 had to move again to be near the front. A site was chosen at Cappy, on a plateau just the other side of the River Somme from Bray-sur-Somme and south of the road to Fontaine-les-Cappy.

Mist and haze hung over the aerodrome on the morning of 21 April

Manfred von Richthofen at Cappy with his dog Moritz. The photograph was taken by *Leutnant* Richard Wenzel of *Jasta* 11, literally only minutes before von Richthofen took off on his last flight.

but von Richthofen was in a good mood. He had scored his 79th and 80th victories the day before, exactly double the number brought down by Oswald Boelcke, who had brought him to *Jasta* 2 less than two years before. Moreover, in less than two weeks it would be his 26th birthday and he was going on leave, hunting in the Black Forest with *Leutnant* Hans Joachim Wolff.

Leutnant Wenzel, one of his pilots was napping on a stretcher and von Richthofen 'accidentally' tipped him over into the mud. Another unsuspecting soul lay down on the empty stretcher and he too suffered the same fate. A chock was tied to the tail of von Richthofen's dog Moritz in playful revenge, causing more laughter from the Baron. The men of *JG* 1 had seldom seen their leader in such good spirits.

The freshening east wind slowly cleared the mist and just after 1030 hours two flights took off, one led by von Richthofen, comprising Hans Joachim Wolff, *Vizefeldwebel* Edgar Scholtz and *Oberleutnant* Walther Karjus and the other by *Leutnant* Hans Weiss. They were to investigate British machines reported flying in the vicinity of the Front.

One after the other the machines landed back at Cappy but there was no sign of von Richthofen. *Hauptmann* Wilhelm Reinhard, who was to succeed von Richthofen in command of *JG* 1, sent out machines to search but to no avail. A sense of shock descended on the aerodrome. Frantic telephone calls were made to observers asking for news of the red triplane. An extraordinary step was taken when a message was sent in clear language to the British requesting information.

That evening *Oberleutnant* Bodenschatz, adjutant of *Jagdgeschwader* 1, travelled to Courtrai, where von Richthofen's father was the local commandant, to inform him that his son was missing. A telegram was also sent to his mother and brother. Hope was maintained that he was a prisoner of war, as the triplane had been seen to make a good landing. Hope was dashed some days later when a British aeroplane dropped a message container on the German side, in which there was a message confirming his death and a photograph of the grave.

Von Richthofen's loss was an enormous psychological blow not only to the German Air Service but to the nation as a whole. (For details of the last flight and his death go to the Morlancourt Ridge entry at the end of Chapter Two.)

While at Cappy *JG* 1 suffered a number of casualties. *Leutnant* Hans Weiss *Jasta* 11, Vizefeldwebel Edgar Scholtz *Jasta* 11, *Leutnant* Hans Joachim Wolff *Jasta* 11, *Unteroffizier* Robert Eiserbeck *Jasta* 11 and Sergeant Otto Schmutzler *Jasta* 4, were all killed and are now buried at Vermandovillers German Cemetery. (See the Vermandovillers German Cemetery entry later in the chapter.)

Latter days at Cappy

During the Allied advance of August 1918 Cappy was one of the aerodromes taken over by the RAF. The history of 24 Squadron RAF recorded on 8 September:

We sent out a patrol in the morning which bagged several Huns and afterwards landed at Cappy, whither '46' and ourselves moved during the morning. (It set in to rain soon after we got there and did not stop for four days.) No hangars or mess tent were up, and there was no cover within miles, not even a tree. I have recollections of Hazell leaning up against a post with a sheet of corrugated iron leaning up against the other side to keep the rain off him. He vowed to buy a shooting stick and umbrella next time he went on leave.

However the tent party got a small mess tent up by the evening and we succeeded in having a regular Piccadilly dinner with fizz and filleted sole, which Sgt. Welch, who was in charge of our mess from start to finish, managed to produce. The machines had to remain out in the wet for a couple of nights. This is one of von Richthofen's old aerodromes, and the road through is labelled 'Richthofen Strasse', while his name is appended to various notices warning people from exploring the machinegun butts. The place is full of very fine dug-outs - some 40 feet deep, and is surrounded by the old 1916 trench lines. Everywhere is littered ammunition of all kinds.

SE5a B8401 'C' of 24 Squadron having its guns aligned at Cappy.

Captain D R MacLaren DSO, MC and Bar, DFC in his Camel F2137 'U' of 46 Squadron probably at Cappy. He claimed the last nine of his fifty-four victories in this aeroplane. It was also the machine in which he searched for the crash site of his commanding officer, Major A H O'Hara-Wood, on 4 October 1918.

Continue along the D164 and pass the sugar factory on your right. At the cross roads turn right along the D71 for a kilometre then turn left on the D71E into Fontaine-les-Cappy. Turn left at the Rue de Fay and continue on the D71E to Foucaucourt-en-Santerre. Cross the N29 and follow the sign to Vermandovillers. The German cemetery is on the left just after crossing over the motorway.

Vermandovillers German Cemetery

This is another very large cemetery, with over 22,600 graves. At the back there is a *Kameradengrab* containing 13,200 casualties and the names of the known are recorded on flat bronze panels. The graves we have come to see are in Plot 2, halfway down on the left side.

The flying casualties here are from units based at nearby aerodromes, as you would expect. There are three from *Jasta* 34b, two from *Jasta* 37 and one from *Jasta* 77b, all based at Foucaucourt. In addition there are five burials from units at Cappy.

Jagdgeschwader 1 remained at Cappy until 27 May, when they transferred further south to support the German 7 *Armee* offensive against the French on the Aisne. In the month or so following von Richthofen's death they suffered five fatalities - four from *Jasta* 11 and one from *Jasta* 4. Of these casualties, Hans Weiss, Hans Joachim Wolff and Edgar Scholtz, were all in the fateful patrol on 21 April when von Richthofen was killed.

Leutnant Hans Weiss *Jasta* 11 (2/1945)

Weiss was born on 19 April 1892, in Hof, near the Austrian border and flew initially with *FA(A)* 282 as an NCO from September 1916 until July 1917. After training at the *Jastaschule*, southeast of Valenciennes, he was posted to *Jasta* 41. In November 1917 he was commissioned and after claiming ten victories was posted to *Jasta* 10.

Von Richthofen toured the schools and other units talent spotting and obviously saw potential in Weiss. It makes you wonder how other *Jagdstaffel* leaders felt about their pilots being poached. In early April Ernst Udet, the leader of *Jasta* 11, had to leave due to ear trouble and Weiss was appointed in his place. Udet was Germany's highest scoring ace to survive the war, with 62 victories and subsequently figured in an incident with 24 Squadron. (See the Latter Days section of the Bertangles Aerodrome entry in Chapter One.)

On 21 April Weiss was awarded the Knight's Cross of the Royal Hohenzollern House Order, which was usually a precursor for the award of the *Pour le Mérite*. In fact, after Weiss' death it was learned that he was indeed about to receive this award. This was unusual at this stage of the war, as a minimum of 20 victories was considered the yardstick for this decoration and Weiss only had eighteen. The *Pour le Mérite* could not be awarded posthumously.

Jasta 11 ran into their nemesis again on 2 May 1918, when they encountered Captain M S Taylor leading a flight of 209 Squadron Camels. A member of the patrol was 'Wop' May, who had narrowly escaped being von Richthofen's 81st victory less than two weeks before. The 209 Squadron combat report described the action thus:

> *Flight dived on eight E.A. at 7,000 ft. just south of Cérisy and I got a burst into several at close range. One white E.A., into which I got a burst at about 20 yards range, turned over on its back and went out of control. This machine was seen to crash by Lieut. Redgate, also confirmed by 65 Squadron.*

Leutnant Hans Weiss, *Jasta* 11. Note the rear of his machine is painted white.

Weiss flew a predominantly white Fokker triplane (*weiss* being the German word for white) and was seen by his comrades to go down and crash north of Méricourt-sur-Somme. One of the other members of the unit immediately drove to the crash site but Weiss was dead, having one shot through the head and another piercing the flying badge on the left side of his jacket. Weiss was buried in the Hero's Cemetery on the aerodrome at Cappy.

Merril Samuel Taylor from Regina, Saskatchewan, was born on 15 April 1893. He had joined the RNAS in early 1917 and failed his initial training course at Cranwell, though he passed the second time. He possibly had a non-flying problem, as his report said at Cranwell; *a very good pilot, a good officer when graduated.*

His first posting like most RNAS pilots was to Dunkirk where he was adjudged a *very good and fearless pilot.*

By the summer of 1918 he was an experienced fighter pilot. Unfortunately his luck ran out on 7 July 1918, when 209 Squadron was involved in a dogfight over Warfusée and lost two machines, including Taylor's. He was seen to go down in a spiral from 1,500 feet and crash near Hamel. The enemy shelled the wreckage, which was abandoned. He has no known grave and is commemorated on the Air Services Memorial at Arras.

Hans Joachim Wolff *Jasta* 11 (2/1942)

Wolff was born on 24 September 1895, in Mulhausen and served initially with *FA(A)* 216 before joining *Jagdstaffel* 11 on 6 July 1917. Despite joining this elite unit, Wolff failed to claim an enemy machine until 18 March 1918, nearly eight months after he arrived. Normally, if a pilot failed to score a victory within a short time he was ruthlessly posted out. Wolff or *Wölffchen*, (little Wolf), was undoubtedly von Richthofen's favourite. Wolff was not lacking in offensive spirit, frequently returning with his machine shot about, resulting in his being wounded on 14 August and 23 November 1917. Von Richthofen obviously saw potential and this faith was rewarded on 18 March 1918, when Wolff brought down his first enemy machine. This first victim was Anthony McCudden, the younger brother of the famous British ace Jimmy McCudden, and a rising star in 84 Squadron. (See the St Souplet British Cemetery entry in Chapter One of *Airfields and Airmen: Cambrai*.) Within a very short time Wolff had claimed ten Allied machines.

On 21 April 1918, together with Wolfram von Richthofen (Manfred's cousin), Walther Kajus and Edgar Scholtz, Wolff followed

The original graves on Cappy aerodrome. Left to right are: Eiserbeck, Weiss, Scholtz and Wolff.

The graves of Wolff, and Eiserbeck, in 2001. The photograph attached to the cross is believed to be of Robert Eiserbeck.

Von Richthofen out on his last fatal flight. During the epic dogfight with 209 Squadron, Wolff was probably the last person in *Jasta* 11 to see the Red Baron alive. During a gap in the dogfight he noticed his leader at extremely low altitude over the River Somme behind a British machine and wondered why he was following his victim so far on the other side. His attention was drawn away by more gunfire from a British machine and when he was able to disengage himself the red triplane had disappeared from view.

When it became clear that von Richthofen was not going to return Wolff was inconsolable, as he felt he should have protected his hero's tail during the dive after the Camel. On 2 May, von Richthofen's 26th birthday, Wolff attended a memorial service in Berlin and, after pouring out his soul to von Richthofen's mother, even she was unable to console him.

Wolff claimed another three British machines but on the morning of 16 May 1918, he was shot down and killed north of Lamotte, just east of Villers-Bretonneux, with two bullets below the heart. Some sources say he was shot down by Captain H D Barton of 24 Squadron, but there is some doubt about this. In the history of *Jagdgeschwader* 1, entitled

Jagd in Flanderns Himmel, written by the adjutant, Karl Bodenschatz, the time is given as 0820 hours and Barton claimed a triplane at 1915 hours - almost exactly twelve hours difference. There are a number of occasions in the book where the times are twelve hours different and are perhaps errors in noting a.m. or p.m. This highlights the difficulty of the researcher in trying to match claims and losses, as there are no German records available to confirm the time in Bodenschatz' book. This important volume has been published in English in recent years as *Hunting with Richthofen*. (See the Further Reading section.)

Whatever the speculation regarding who brought down Wolff, he was buried in an honoured grave on the aerodrome at Cappy and was subsequently moved to the present German cemetery at Vermandovillers.

Robert Eiserbeck and Edgar Scholtz (2/1943 and 2/1940)

Interred in the same grave as Hans Joachim Wolff is *Unteroffizier* Robert Eiserbeck, also of *Jasta* 11, killed when shot down on 12 April 1918. On my last visit to the cemetery their grave was adorned with a photograph, obviously placed there by a relative, and it is believed to be of Robert Eiserbeck.

Buried alongside Wolff is *Vizefeldwebel* Edgar Scholtz, who also

The triplanes of *Jasta* 11 on Lechelle aerodrome in early April 1918. The three pilots in the foreground are, from left to right: Robert Eiserbeck, Hans Weiss and Edgar Scholtz. Scholtz is wearing the harness of a Heinecke parachute, the first of which had reached *JG* 1 in early March.

flew in von Richthofen's last flight and was killed on the aerodrome the same day as Weiss. He stalled on take off and crashed to the ground. Scholtz had already survived one harrowing incident when, during a dogfight, a falling Albatros had crashed into him, knocking his tail off. His triplane fell several thousands of feet but he miraculously emerged from the crash unscathed. A rising star in the *Staffel*, he had claimed six Allied machines before his career came to an abrupt end. An hour after his death, notification came through of Scholtz' promotion to *Leutnant der Reserve*.

For further information concerning the careers of German fighter pilots, I recommend The *Jasta* Pilots by Franks, Bailey and Duiven.

Return to the N29 at Foucaucourt and turn left towards Amiens. Just after leaving the village there is a municipal cemetery on the left. Stop here, making sure your vehicle is off the very busy road.

Foucaucourt Aerodrome

From the cemetery the German aerodrome occupied the large grass area on the other side of the road.

Foucaucourt had been used as an advanced landing ground by the RFC in early 1918 but, as the Germans advanced in March 1918, it was

Foucaucourt Aerodrome

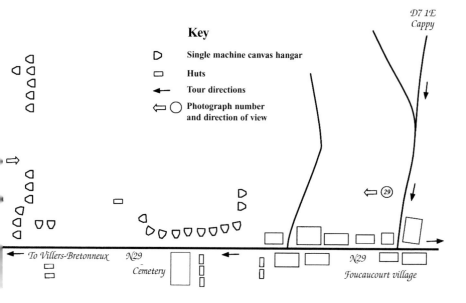

Picture No. 28. Foucaucourt aerodrome looking east towards the village.

abandoned. In late 1918 with the Allied advance this was another of the sites employed to keep up with the retreating German army. Whether the British and German aerodromes were the same site is impossible to say, but it is very likely so.

Jastas 16b, 34b, 37 and 77b were based here from March until the end of July 1918. The German army was predominantly a Prussian one, though other states had large contingents. In addition to the suffix b for Bavaria already mentioned, certain other states such as Württemberg, and Saxony were able to establish their own flying units. These were identified by the suffixes of w for Württemberg and s for Saxony. In October 1918 a Bavarian *Jagdgeschwader*, No. IV, comprising *Jastas* 23b, 32b, 34b and 35b, was established.

Picture No. 29. Foucaucourt aerodrome , a view to the west. The cemetery can be seen on the left of the road.

Rudolph Stark of *Jasta* 34b

Rudolph Stark, whom we met in the Fricourt entry, where he described the funeral of Walter Ewers, commanding officer of *Jasta* 77, was a pilot in *Jasta* 34b. He described the aerodrome at Foucaucourt in his autobiography *Wings of War* thus:

22.4.18. A new aerodrome has been found for us. It is much nearer the front, on the huge straight road and close to Foucaucourt. We migrate thither; one after the other, our various accessories are brought up from Bouvincourt, and the removal is soon finished. The Bavarian Jagdstaffel, No. 77, lies next to us, while a Prussian Jagdstaffel occupies the other end of the ground. We are not far from Cappy, the headquarters of Richthofen's squadron. At first we find our starts and landings on the new ground rather difficult because of the numerous shell-holes on its surface. Our aerodrome squads have their hands full filling in the holes and trenches.

We are living in a desert. Not a house to be seen anywhere. Many villages have completely disappeared. The only signs of them are boards at wayside crosses on which is inscribed in English: "This was Villers Carbone! This was Vendelles!" Everywhere I see new and old graves.

Near the aerodrome there is a small wood of beeches and alders. We have cut a way through its wild undergrowth and put up our tents and corrugated iron huts in its midst.

Twelve of us inhabit one hut. Our beds stand in rows; we stumble over trunks and twist our devious ways past our neighbours. This does not worry us so much, because we can always behave in neighbourly fashion, but our animals are not quite so amenable.

Some of us have dogs , one owns a cat, another has brought three magpies along, while yet another has caught a fox-cub. All

Rudolf Stark and his Fokker Triplane.

German canvas hangars on the aerodrome at Foucaucourt.

this menagerie has to be parked in the one hut, over and under the beds, thus curtailing the space available for humans. Unfortunately all the dogs are at war with one another in addition to cherishing the most evil intentions towards the cat. The latter lies in ambush for the magpies, with the result that we often arrive home in the middle of a scrap and just in time to prevent a tragedy. The fox-cub is the only one that sits good and quiet in his corner, but he gets so bored that he goes and grabs everyone's boots in turn and gnaws them. Owing to the presence of the aforesaid menagerie the air in our hut is not exactly what one would call pure ozone.

Thank the Lord, the weather is good, so we can spend the greater part of the day in the open air. We have a lot of flying every day, and in the evening we are so tired that we do not care where we sleep.

The bombing of German aerodromes

By 1918 tactics had changed for the RAF. Long gone were the days of sending out 'penny packet' formations. Patrols had become larger and it was not unusual for an operation to be carried out by an entire wing. Not only were many squadron commanders flying patrols but also senior officers, like Lieutenant Colonel Louis Strange, were actually leading their wings. Strange had six squadrons under his command with over 100 aircraft. During the summer of 1918 there was a systematic bombing campaign against German targets, including aerodromes. One of these large operations against Foucaucourt was described by Sholto Douglas, commanding 84 Squadron, in his book *Years of Combat*:

There was one occasion in the middle of July, 1918, when I wished fervently that we could have been let off the leash. It was a good example of the way in which the planners were taking double precautions in protecting the aircraft doing the bombing, while at the same time wasting the time of the fighters. Wing Headquarters ordered a raid on the German aerodrome at Foucaucourt, the way to which was indicated by the perfectly

178

straight road that runs due east from Amiens to St Quentin. By air it was less than thirty miles away, and the instructions given to the five squadrons involved were that they should carry out "the destruction of hangars and machines and the infliction of as many casualties as possible".

We set out, three of the five squadrons coming from Bertangles, with the SE5's providing the fighter escort for the Camels which were to do the bombing and ground strafing. On this occasion I led the fifteen SE5's of 84 Squadron. The fighters were stepped up in the sky to a height of about eighteen thousand feet. In a way the whole operation was a forerunner of the fighter sweeps we were to stage over northern France in the second war twenty-three years later.

When we arrived over the aerodrome at Foucaucourt, the Camels dived down on their targets, dropping their bombs and going about generally shooting-up everything in sight. My job was to keep my squadron up as top cover of the escort, and we sat up there watching the havoc being caused by the attacking Camels. I saw two direct hits by bombs on some hangars and at least six more hits on various huts, and I saw a Fokker biplane on the ground demolished by another direct hit.

During all this I was keeping a sharp look-out for German fighters because I fully expected that the Huns would be stirred up enough to try and retaliate by jumping on those low-flying Camels. But for once not a single Hun appeared. Even archie was pretty innocuous, high up, because the German gunners were paying most of their attentions to the squadrons lower down. I had rather looked forward to being able to leap on the Huns, since we were at the top of the escort, with my squadron packed in behind me, and when none appeared I longed to go off and find them. But there we had to stay, high up and looking on, and just waiting.

In *Airfields and Airmen; Ypres* on page 79 there is an incident in which Lieutenant Colonel W F MacNeece, commanding 5 Kite Balloon Wing, was shot down and injured by a 'friendly' SE5. Douglas was in the immediate vicinity when this occurred and suspicion fell heavily on him. Only when he produced a certificate, signed by his squadron Armament Officer to the effect he had not fired his guns on the patrol, was he able to clear his name. Sholto Douglas visited the unfortunate MacNeece in hospital to explain what had happened during his patrol, but due to concussion the latter did not really understand. In the mid-1920s, when they were both serving at the Air Ministry, Douglas was able to give a full explanation. However, he was never quite certain that MacNeece was fully convinced.

The aerodrome changes hands

In the late summer of 1918, during the Allied advance, the aerodrome was occupied by Nos. 8, 73, 85 and 208 Squadrons RAF. Chris Draper, commanding 208 Squadron, described his new aerodrome in the history of 208 Squadron, *Naval Eight*, and found it in much the same condition that Stark had:

> *We left Tramecourt and the 10th Wing, with which the Squadron had been for sixteen months, on the 29th September, 1918, for the 22nd Wing and went to Foucaucourt, right on the Somme. After the green fields and trees of the unspoilt area around Tramecourt, the desolation of the Somme was a terrific contrast. The Hun having to retreat, we were advancing over the most blasted, barren and shell-ridden country imaginable; the so-called aerodromes were just old battlefields with the shell holes filled in, and for miles there wasn't a tree or building other than an Army hut.*

Readers will remember in *Airfields and Airmen:Ypres* that Chris Draper had suffered the unenviable task of burning all his squadron's Sopwith Camels at La Gorgue. They had been caught on the ground in thick fog during the German advance of spring 1918.

Continue along the N29 towards Amiens and after approximately one kilometre turn right on the D329 to Proyart. Opposite Proyart church turn left on the D41 signposted to Harbonnières. After 100 metres turn right along an unclassified and unsignposted road. Pass through Morcourt and as you arrive in Cerisy you will see the green CWGC signs. Follow the signs and park in front of the French cemetery.

Cerisy-Gailly Military Cemetery

To get to Cerisy Gailly Miltary Cemetery you have walk through the French National Cemetery and the British extension at the back. A grass path connects the other British plot to the south. We have come here to visit the grave of John Joseph Petre, who was commanding officer of No. 6 (Naval) Squadron attached to the RFC. His grave (I D39) is at the back of the cemetery. It is the very last burial in a row.

The observant visitor will notice the spelling of squadron on his headstone.

This was the site of 13 and 39 Casualty Clearing Stations and then the 41st Stationary Hospital from May 1917 until March 1918. The original name of the burial ground (9/120) was the New French Cemetery. There were 158 French and 35 Germans buried here but they have been removed leaving nearly 750 casualties.

Number 6 (Naval) Squadron

The unit was formed on 1 November 1916, by re-designating 'A' Squadron of No. 4 Wing as No. 6 (Naval). On 15 March 1917, it was sent down to join the 13 (Army) Wing in the Third Army area to reinforce the RFC for the forthcoming Battle of Arras. Equipped with French Nieuport scouts, it was based at Bellevue, twelve kilometres northeast of Doullens, on the road to Arras. Commanded by Jack Petre, it joined a number of other naval units attached to the RFC.

Squadron Commander John Joseph Petre (I D39)

Jack Petre was born on 11 April 1894, and was a remarkable sportsman at school, playing full back in the school football team and winning several athletic cups, including one for best all-round athlete. In April 1914 he won the solo motorcycle Public School Race at Brooklands. At school he had been very interested in flying, though his brother Edward had been killed in a flying accident. On 17 September 1914, he joined the RNAS and gained his pilot's certificate, No. 942, in October 1914 at Eastbourne.

Posted to Dunkirk, he was involved in bombing Ostend and Zeebrugge, as well as coastal reconnaissance. He was twice Mentioned in Despatches for attacks on sheds at Ostend and for work with the Dover Patrol, while with 1 Wing. In June 1916 he was awarded the DSC and then in October received the French *Croix de Guerre* for bringing down a German machine. On 22 October he had attacked an LVG in his Nieuport scout and its destruction was confirmed by a Belgian pilot.

J J Petre, commanding No. 6 Naval Squadron, killed on 13 April 1917.

Petre was yet another of the many non-operational casualties that occurred in the flying services. A simple accident resulted in the death of an exceptional pilot. Friday, 13 April 1917, was indeed an unlucky day for him. One of the officers in his squadron described his crash:

The accident occurred at 11.50 yesterday, April 13th, when he went up to practise firing at a target on the ground. He did one dive from about 1,500 feet to about 200, and appeared to flatten out rather quickly. He then climbed up again, did a very steep bank, and then started to dive again. After diving two or three hundred feet the machine broke in the air, and the result was fatal.

Another officer wrote:

It appears that he had a good many raw pilots in his squadron, and in order to give them confidence he had been doing a good deal of flying himself. On the day he was killed he had been doing spiral nose dives, when apparently without any warning both wings snapped off sharp and he fell about three hundred feet.

Jack Petre (right) in front of a naval Nieuport scout. Note the over wing mounted Lewis machine gun.

The Nieuport scout was prone to lower wing collapses. The rectangular main spar of the lower wing passed through the circular fitting at the bottom of the V strut joining the upper and lower wings. Packing pieces were inserted between the spar and the circular fitting.The effects of changes in humidity on the packing pieces, which were often made of poorly seasoned timber, meant that the fitting could become loose. This would allow the wing to rotate in the socket. Once the wing had turned sufficiently for it to be face on to the slipstream, it would then fold and probably detach, with usually fatal results. Mick Mannock was one of the few to survive an incident where the upper wing did not collapse as well and he was able to land with a bottom wing completely missing.

Nieuport Scout number N3102 of No. 6 Naval Squadron. The socket at the base of the V strut, between upper and lower wings, caused problems in the early days.

Petre was buried initially in the village cemetery at Dernancourt and later transferred to Cerisy-Gailly.

Continue along the Rue de Cimetière to the T junction and turn right along the D71. After approximately two kilometres turn right on the D42 signposted to Sailly-Laurette. At the church in Sailly-Laurette turn left along the D233 (this is the D42E on some maps) towards Sailly-le-Sec. After about 200 metres turn right on the C3 and continue until the CWGC sign to Dive Copse Cemetery.

Dive Copse Military Cemetery

The grave of G H Harding (I D7) is at the far right of the cemetery (9/113) and is in a distinctive group of three headstones.

During the Somme battle of 1916 a number of Field Ambulances were concentrated here, which became XIV Corps Main Dressing Station. A small wood nearby was known as Dive Copse, after the officer commanding the Main Dressing Station. There are nearly 600 casualties buried in the cemetery.

George Helliwell Harding (I D7)

I first came to this cemetery out of idle curiosity, after visiting the von Richthofen crash site and discovered that one of his last victims is buried here. In fact it is one of life's little ironies that if you stand by Harding's grave you can actually see the spot where von Richthofen was killed.

The 79 Squadron crest. Motto: Nil Nobis Obstare Potest (Nothing Can Withstand Us).

Harding, born two days before Christmas in 1893, was an American from Minneapolis. When the United States entered the war he tried to enlist in the army, but would have had to wait due to the avalanche of men volunteering. Anxious to join up he travelled to Canada and enlisted in the RFC. He was a gifted pilot and after qualifying was held back to instruct other pupils. Eventually he was able to get himself sent to the war and

Sopwith Dolphin H7244 'S' of 79 Squadron, displaying the squadron marking of a white square.

arrived in England in August 1917. A further frustrating delay was caused by advanced training with a number of units in the UK. Eventually he realised his ambition and was posted to France, arriving at 79 Squadron based at Estrée-Blanche on 2 March 1918. The squadron moved three times in March, keeping ahead of the advancing German army, including just two days at Cachy. On 24 March they moved to Beauvois and it was from here that Harding took off on the morning of 27 March for his last flight.

Von Richthofen had already shot down two British machines on this day and Harding was to be the third. In his combat report he wrote:

> Soon after I had shot down my 72nd opponent in flames, I attacked once more with the same gentlemen of the Jasta. Just then I observed that one of my gentlemen was attacked by a Bristol Fighter. I put myself behind this machine and shot him down in flames from a distance of 50 metres.
>
> I noticed that there was only one occupant. The observer's seat was blocked and I surmise it was filled with bombs. I first killed the pilot; the machine was caught on the propeller. I fired a few more shots and the plane then burned and broke up in the air; the fuselage fell into a small wood and continued to burn.

Why von Richthofen thought a Bristol Fighter was flying around without an observer is difficult to understand. He was in fact encountering a Sopwith Dolphin for the first time - the type had only been at the front for two months. With its back staggered wings, and with two pairs of struts each side, it did have the appearance of a two-seater.

Harding had only served with 79 Squadron for twenty-five days and had the misfortune to meet the vastly experienced and deadly von Richthofen.

In 1919 Harding's sister was entertaining troops in France and set out to locate her brother's grave. Finding a small graveyard, with a number of unidentified graves, she persuaded the Imperial War Graves Commission (as it was then called) to disinter the remains. After identifying her brother, his remains were removed to Dive Copse. Her courage can only be imagined, as having been shot down in flames and spent a year buried on a battlefield, identification would have been traumatic to say the least. The family inscription on his headstone is very moving: *That their dust may rebuild a nation and their souls relight a star.*

The Red Baron, though, was only to survive another month himself, before being killed within sight of his 73rd victim's grave.

Continue north to the D1 and turn right to Bray-sur-Somme. In the town centre turn left by the church onto the D329 towards Albert. After about a kilometre and just before the small airstrip on the right, turn left onto the C6 signposted to Etinehem. Turn right at the Grove Town Cemetery sign.

Grove Town Military Cemetery

The first grave we have come to visit (I C39) is just to the right of the cemetery entrance. The other grave (III A19) is just to the right of the Stone of Remembrance and is one of a distinctive pair of headstones.

This cemetery (9/107), like so many others, was the site of Casualty Clearing Stations and was used for casualties in the 1916 Somme battle. The Casualty Clearing Stations were moved in April 1917 and, apart from a few burials in August and September, the cemetery was effectively closed. One of the two graves we are here to visit was the result of an odd accident.

C E N Cooper 6 Kite Balloon Section (I C39)

On the morning of 16 September 1916, FE2b No. 6971 of 18 Squadron left an advanced HQ field to carry out a patrol on the Fourth Army front. It was crewed by Second Lieutenants T L Hayward and P J Smyth. Only the day before, while flying with another pilot, Smyth had been shot down uninjured by ground fire. They had been flying at low level trying to read a ground signalling shutter device near Flers and had their controls, radiator and fuel tanks shot through by machine gun fire. The machine had to be dismantled and towed away during the night to avoid the unwelcome attention of German artillery fire.

Smyth's luck was not to continue. While returning from patrol on 16 September the FE2b flew headlong into the

Lieutenant C E N Cooper, kite balloon observer accidentally killed on 16 September 1916.

cable of one of 6 Kite Balloon Section's kite balloons. The cable parted and the observer, Lieutenant C E N Cooper, was killed. The FE crashed and was almost totally destroyed. The only items salvaged were the rudder, tail fin, petrol tanks and nine struts. The engine crankshaft was buried eighteen inches in the ground and even one of the Lewis machine guns was smashed. Smyth died in a dressing station of his injuries the following day. Hayward, the pilot, miraculously survived, though badly injured. Smyth is buried in Corbie Communal Cemetery Extension in Plot 2, Row D, Grave 58.

During the Second World War balloons were not used for observation but were employed in large numbers to form barrages around important targets such as the city of London. The cables in the barrage were intended to bring down German aeroplanes in much the same way as the Hayward and Smyth accident.

James Dacres Belgrave (III A19)

Belgrave, the son of a barrister in the Inner Temple, was born in 1895. He came from Chinnor in Oxfordshire and after attending the Royal Military College at Sandhurst saw service in France with the Ox and Bucks Light Infantry. In the late

Captain J D Belgrave MC.

summer of 1916 he was seconded to the RFC and qualified as a pilot, before being posted to 45 Squadron. His squadron was operating the Sopwith 11/2 Strutter and suffering heavy losses. Despite flying a hopelessly outclassed machine, over the next six months Belgrave and his observers claimed six German aeroplanes shot down, for which he was awarded a Military Cross.

Returning to England he served with 37 and 61 Home Defence Squadrons, twice engaging Gotha bombers without success. On 19 April 1918, he returned to the Western Front for a second tour of duty, as a flight commander with 60 Squadron, this time flying the SE5a. They were based at Boffles, northwest of Doullens. Sixty Squadron had a proud record, as Albert Ball VC had served in it during 1916 and then in 1917 Billy Bishop had won a VC while with the unit after claiming nearly 40 German machines.

It took a while for Belgrave to settle down and he was not to claim an enemy machine until a month after his arrival. In just under four weeks from the middle of May to the middle of June, though, he shot down another eleven German aircraft and was awarded a Bar to his MC. Unfortunately, on 13 June 1918, he went missing in unexplained circumstances.

He and three other SE5s took off at the unearthly hour of four o'clock in the morning for a patrol. They dived on an enemy two-seater four miles east of Albert, driving it down out of control. Belgrave was last seen following it down into the cloud. The enemy machine was seen to crash by an anti-aircraft battery but Belgrave failed to return. Whether he was hit by the gunner of the two-seater or was brought down by ground fire remains a mystery.

Another member of the patrol, Henry Gordon, a Canadian from Durham, Ontario, was on his first sortie. Despite his total inexperience, upon seeing Lieutenant R G Lewis force land behind the German lines due to engine failure, he very gallantly landed near him. A number of German soldiers arrived and opened fire. Gordon ran back to his machine, calling for Lewis to follow him. The latter though, walked towards the enemy party, presumably to allow Gordon to make his escape. Once airborne Gordon circled the scene but was unable to fire on the enemy, due to the fact they had surrounded the hapless Lewis. Gordon returned with his machine shot about by ground fire. His selfless act surely deserved some recognition but none was forthcoming. He failed to return from a patrol little more than a month later and was later reported as killed in action. The fourth member of the patrol, Lieutenant John MacVicker, was killed later the same month.

It is a sobering fact that of the four pilots in the patrol only one, R G Lewis, who was made prisoner of war, survived the Great War.

Return to the D329 and turn left to Albert. This concludes the third and final tour of *Airfields and Airmen: Somme*.

Conclusion

Since the publication of *Airfields and Airmen: Ypres* the address of the membership secretary of Cross and Cockade International - The First World War Aviation Historical Society has changed. For those readers whose interest in First World War aviation may have been aroused by this present book I can recommend joining this excellent society. The address is:

Membership Secretary
Cross and Cockade International
5 Cave Drive
Downend
Bristol BS16 2TL.

Their website is http://www.crossandcockade.com

In addition, I am always interested in contacting First World War aviators or their relatives, whether they figure in the *Airfields or Airmen* series of books or not. My e-mail address is oconnor@stonehousecottage.freeserve.co.uk

FURTHER READING

A Selected Bibliography

Courage Remembered, Kingsley Ward and E Gibson, HMSO 1989.

The Sky Their Battlefield, Trevor Henshaw, Grub Street 1995.

Airmen Died in the Great War, Chris Hobson, Hayward and Son 1995.

Max Immelmann, Eagle of Lille, Franz Immelmann, John Hamilton Ltd, no date.

Aviation Awards of Imperial Germany in World War 1, Vols 1 - 6, Neal W O'Connor, Foundation for Aviation World War 1, 1988 - 1999.

Under the Guns of the German Aces, N Franks and H Giblin, Grub Street 1997.

Fokker EIII, Windsock Datafile No. 15, Peter Grosz, Albatros Publications 1989.

Naval Eight, edited by E G Johnstone, Arms and Armour Press 1972.

Vickers FB5, Windsock Datafile No. 56, J M Bruce, Albatros Publications 1996.

Observer, A J Insall, William Kimber and Co 1970.

Sopwith Scout 7309, Sir Gordon Taylor, Cassell and Co 1968.

Albert Ball VC, Chaz Bowyer, William Kimber and Co 1977.

Sagittarius Rising, Cecil Lewis, Peter Davies 1936.

For Valour The Air VC's, Chaz Bowyer, William Kimber and Co 1978.

High in the Empty Blue, The History of 56 Squadron RFC/RAF 1916-1919, Alex Revell, Flying Machines Press 1995.

Years of Combat, Sholto Douglas, Collins 1963.

Flying Corps Headquarters 1914-18, Maurice Baring, William Heinemann 1930.

Maurice Baring, A Citizen of Europe, Emma Letley, Constable and Co 1991.

Escape Fever, Geoffrey Harding, John Hamilton Ltd 1935.

Airco DH2, Windsock Datafile No. 48, B J Gray, Albatros Publications 1994.

The Red Air Fighter, M von Richthofen, The Aeroplane and General Publishing Co 1918.

The Red Knight of Germany, Floyd Gibbons, Cassell 1930.

Hawker VC, Tyrrel M Hawker, Mitre Press 1965.

A History of 24 Squadron Royal Air Force, A E Illingworth, The Aeroplane and General Publishing Co 1920.

Ace of the Iron Cross, Ernst Udet, Newnes 1937.

The Fated Sky, Sir Philip Joubert de la Ferté, Hutchinson and Co 1952.

Chasing the Wind, K R van der Spuy, Books of Africa 1966.

The Storks, N Franks and F Bailey, Grub Street 1998.

I Flew with the Lafayette Escadrille, Edwin C Parsons, E C Seale and Co 1963.

The Lafayette Flying Corps, J N Hall and C B Nordhoff, Houghton Mifflin Co 1920.

Private Memorials of the Great War on the Western Front, Barry Thorpe, The Western Front Association, 1999.

Recipients of the DCM 1914-1920, R W Walker, Midland Medals 1981.

I Flew a Camel, Curtis Kinney, Dorrance and Co 1972.

The Red Baron's Last Flight, N Franks and A Bennett, Grub Street 1997.

Wings of War, Rudolf Stark, John Hamilton Ltd 1933.

The Distinguished Flying Medal. A Record of Courage 1918-1982, I T Tavender, J B Hayward and Son 1990.

Pictorial History of the German Army Air Service, Alex Imrie, Ian Allan 1971.

The Royal Flying Corps in France, Ralph Barker (Two volumes), Constable 1994 and 1995.

The Jasta Pilots, Franks/Bailey/Duiven, Grub Street 1996.

Above the Trenches, Shores/Franks/Guest, Grub Street 1990.

Above the Lines, Franks/Bailey/Guest, Grub Street 1993.

Bloody April, Alan Morris, Jarrolds 1967.

The Balloonatics, Alan Morris, Jarrolds 1970.

The Fokker Triplane, Alex Imrie, Arms and Armour 1992.

The Mad Major, Major Christopher Draper DSC, Air Review Ltd 1962.

The Aeroplanes of the Royal Flying Corps (Military Wing), J M Bruce, Putnams 1982.

INDEX
A Selective Index

Acland, Second Lieutenant W H D, 51

Aerodromes
Abeele, 81
Amiens, 101, 104, 107, 110, 111
Bailleul, 88
Baisieux, 49
Bar le Duc, 121
Beauvois, 184
Boffles, 186
Boistrancourt, 30
Brooklands, 111, 132, 163
Cachy, 101, 114, 120, 122, 131, 145, 184
Cappy, 12, 149, 163-170, 172, 174
Conteville, 95
Courcelles-le-Comte, 42
Dover, 111
Eastchurch, 38
Estrée Blanche, 184
Farnborough, 111, 132
Fienvillers, 98
Flesselles, 65
Foucaucourt,124, 149, 156, 175-180
Glisy, 106
La Gorgue, 180
Lechelle, 167,174
Le Crotoy, 129
Le Quesnoy, 132
Luxeuil, 119, 121
Mariakerke, 39
Maubeuge, 110, 111
Netheravon, 111, 112, 129
Poulainville, 60, 68, 71
Proyart East, 162
Shoreham, 29
St Denis Westrem, 66
St Omer, 9, 77, 78
Suttons Farm, 77
Treizennes, 98
Vert Galand, 9, 27, 37, 39, 45-47 ,49, 50, 52, 54, 56, 69, 82, 95, 127, 154, 159
Vignacourt, 60
Villers Bocage, 60
Villers-Bretonneux 1915, 98, 101, 126, 127, 161
Villers-Bretonneux 1917, 101, 130, 131
Warloy, 144
Wasquehal, 36

Andrews, Captain J O, 52, 77, 81-84, 87, 88
Archer, Second Lieutenant A E C, 77

Armstrong, Captain D V, 153
Atkinson, Captain E D, 160
Auger, *Capitaine* A, 131

Balcombe-Brown, Major R, 149,158-160
Ball, Captain A, 27, 47, 53-56, 159, 186
Baring, Lieutenant M, 57, 107, 109, 131
Barlow, Airman R K, 111
Barrington-Kennett, Captain B H, 31, 32
Barrington-Kennett, Major V A, 27, 31-34
Barton, Captain H D, 173,174
Bäumer, *Leutnant* P, 166
Beadle, F P H, 111
Beauchamp Proctor, Captain A F W, 92
Belgrave, Captain J D, 186
Bell, Captain D, 141, 142, 144
Bennett, A, 147
Bishop, Captain W A, 186
Blomfield, Major R G, 158-160
Bodenschatz, *Oberleutnant* K, 168, 174
Böhme, *Leutnant* E, 140
Boelcke, *Hauptmann* O, 34, 35, 140, 168
Booker, Major C D, 66-68
Bott, Lieutenant A J, 98
Boyd, Lieutenant W, 144
Brancker, Brigadier General Sir S, 107-109,123
Brocard, *Capitaine* F, 115, 117, 118
Bromet, Squadron Commander G, 37, 39
Brown, Captain A R, 92, 146, 147
Brown, Lieutenant J, 149, 150, 154
Burke, Major C J, 108, 109

Callaghan, Second Lieutenant E C, 102, 103
Callaghan, Major J C, 101, 102
Callaghan, Captain S C, 102
Carmichael, Captain G I, 112

Cemeteries, American
Wareghem, 137

Cemeteries, British
Achiet-le-Grand, 27
Ancre, 27
Bertangles, 27
Corbie, 185
Bronfay Farm, 149, 161

Brown's Copse, 59
Carnoy, 134, 149, 157
Cerisy-Gailly, 149, 180, 183
Contay, 101
Couin, 13, 27, 42
Dive Copse, 149, 183
Doullens, 133
Forceville, 27, 39, 49, 95, 128
Grove Town, 149, 185
Hangard, 101, 122
Longuenesse, 78
Le Touret, 31
Miraumont, 27
Pont du Hem, 30
Porte-de-Paris, 140
Regina Trench, 27, 30
St Souplet, 172
Tincourt, 40
Vermelles, 44
Vignacourt, 27, 60, 65
Villers-Bretonneux, 101, 134, 138

Cemeteries, French
St Acheul, 101, 111

Cemeteries, German
Annouellin, 56
Frasnoy, 99
Fricourt, 94, 149, 177
Vermandovillers, 149, 169, 170, 174

Compston, Major R J O, 38
Cooper, Lieutenant C E N, 185
Crabbe, Second Lieutenant H L B, 134, 158
Creed, Second Lieutenant G S,109
Crutch, Lieutenant J H, 83

Deullin, *Capitaine* A L, 115, 117
Diendl, *Oberleutnant* O, 155
Docherty, Private P, 135, 138
Donald, Air Mechanic T H, 73-76
Dorme, *Sous Lieutenant* R P M, 115, 118
Douglas, Major W S, 56, 92, 137, 178-180
Draper, Major C, 180
Dyke, Sergeant W G, 163

Egerton, Major R, 39-42
Eiserbeck, *Unteroffizier* R, 168, 173, 174
Ewers, *Oberleutnant* W, 155, 156, 177

Fitzgerald, Lieutenant R J, 27, 60-65